LIVING
OUT
LOUD

Anna Quindlen

LIVING
OUT
LOUD

ANNA QUINDLEN

RANDOM HOUSE

NEW YORK

Grateful acknowledgment is made to Irving Music, Inc., for permission
to reprint an excerpt from the lyrics to "Wouldn't It Be Nice" by
Brian Wilson and Tony Asher. Copyright © 1966 Sea of Tunes/Irving
Music, Inc.

Library of Congress Cataloging-in-Publication Data

Quindlen, Anna.
Living out loud.

I. Title.
AC8Q56   1988   081   88-11348
ISBN 0-394-56964-4

Manufactured in the United States of America
2 3 4 5 6 7 8 9
First Edition

Book design by Debbie Glasserman

FOR GERRY,
FOR ALWAYS

To take what there *is*, and use it, without waiting forever in vain for the preconceived—to dig deep into the actual and get something out of *that*—this doubtless is the right way to live.

—HENRY JAMES

ACKNOWLEDGMENTS

t is impossible to write an honest column about your own life without somehow involving your family and your friends. I have tried to do this without unnecessarily invading the privacy of those I love. I hope I have succeeded.

The people whose lives have been most affected by my work are Quindlen and Christopher Krovatin, my sons. During the years these columns were being written, neither of them knew how to read. Someday I hope they will see these essays as affectionate and true memoirs of their childhood. My husband, Gerry Krovatin, has also seen himself in print a little too often for comfort. When I have given speeches about my column, the question I am asked most often is "How does he feel about all this?" Sometimes he likes it, and sometimes he doesn't. But he has always been enormously supportive. So, too, has my father, Robert V. Quindlen. He has been an extraordinary influence on my life and my work.

Many of these columns were the products of long telephone conversations with my friends. I want to thank them: Leslie Bennetts, Cynthia Gorney, Janet Maslin, Richard J. Meislin, Kathy Slobogin, Michael Specter. I also want to thank a friend who is a wonderful agent, Amanda Urban.

This column began in *The New York Times* in May 1986. It was invented by A. M. Rosenthal, then executive editor, and supported by Max Frankel, now executive editor. My editor at *The Times*, Margot Slade, has improved my prose time after time. My editor at Random House, Kate Medina, has taken good care of this book, and of me.

Finally, I want to thank all the people who have written to me during the years when I was doing this column. If it weren't for those letters, I would have quit before I'd barely gotten started.

CONTENTS

IN THE BEGINNING

t was very cold the night my mother died. She was a little older than I am today, a young woman with five young children who had been eaten alive by disease, had wasted away to a wisp, had turned into a handful of bones wound round with pale silk. When my father came home from the hospital we gathered the younger children in his bedroom and tried to tell them what had happened. Naturally we could not; it would be years before we would know ourselves. Perhaps it is some indication of how spectacularly difficult our task was, and how spectacularly we failed at it, that, when we were both adults, my younger sister told me that she had spent five years waiting for our mother to come home from the hospital, where she was certain they would find a way to make her well.

I suppose this is an odd way to begin the story of writing a column of personal reflections, a column that I did not start to write until a full fifteen years after the January evening on which my mother died. And yet it is the beginning. For there are two parts to writing a column about yourself, about your life and your feelings. One is, naturally, the writing itself, the prose and, if you've got it in you, the poetry.

But the other is the living, and that is the harder part. When I was twenty-two, I wanted badly to do such a column, but the managing editor of the newspaper for which I was working said that I was a good enough writer, but that I hadn't lived enough to be qualified for "living out loud." At the time I was enraged by his attitude; now I know he was right. My prose may have been adequate, but my emotional development was not.

It was not until the aftermath of my mother's death that I began to realize that I would have to fashion a life for myself— and that is what I have been trying to do, in a workmanlike way, ever since. This seems rather ordinary to me now, but at the beginning it was odd and frightening. Up until that point life had fashioned me. There had been almost no decisions for me to make, in part because I was not permitted to make them, and in part because I saw no path other than the one I was on. I went to school, did well, came home, ate dinner, finished my homework, went to bed. I fought with my brothers and loved but did not know my parents. I wore what my friends wore and said the kinds of things they said, and if, somewhere, someone was deciding what we should wear and discuss, I did not know who that someone was. There were two good reasons not to interfere with such a life. I felt powerless to do so, and I was happy.

It was a lucky coincidence for me that this impeccable super-structure and my own private frame of reference came tumbling down at about the same time, since I like to take all my medicine at once rather than have it doled out in dribs and drabs. My mother began to die on the cusp of the sixties and the seventies, at the same time that the religion and the rules that had circumscribed her life and mine died, too. And I was left with a self to do with what I pleased. I felt as though someone had handed me a grenade with the pin pulled.

Now I know that I was one among many, that all over America and indeed the world women were beginning to feel this same way, beginning to feel the great blessing and the horrible curse of enormous possibility. "Oh, you girls," an elderly woman once sighed, talking to me of my job and looking down at my belly big with child as we sat together in a nursing home in New York City. "All these choices for you." I smiled, and she sighed. "I feel so sorry for you," she added, and I smiled again, for I knew she was right.

I knew that in the years following that January night I had been numb with fear at some simple truths: that I was going to have to find a way to earn a living, make a decision about what I wanted to do and how to go about doing it, find a home and make it my own. That was the only response I could find to the scent of death, sticking to my clothes, rising from my hair. The house in which my mother had sickened and drawn near to death was sold not long after she died, and so in every sense I was adrift. I felt orphaned, cut off from the past. It was many years before I would know that I had found both feelings liberating.

It was perfectly valid to feel adrift. There were few role models. The women of my mother's generation had, in the main, only one decision to make about their lives: who they would marry. From that, so much else followed: where they would live, in what sort of conditions, whether they would be happy or sad or, so often, a bit of both. There were roles and there were rules. My mother did not work. The money she spent was earned by my father. Her children arrived as nature saw fit. I assumed that she never used birth control, although when I was eighteen she set me straight. "Yes, we did," she said. "Rhythm."

My father often says today that he believes their marriage would have been sorely tried by the changes which became my birthright. And I think he is right. When I was younger and saw the world in black and white, I believed the woman my mother was was determined by her character, not by social conditions. Now that I see only shades of gray, I know that that is nonsense. She would have gotten her second wind in the seventies. She would have wanted the things I have come to take for granted: work, money, a say in the matter, a voice of her own. She would have wanted to run her life, too. Instead she was born and died in an era in which her life ran her.

I have rarely felt that way about my own life. I have mostly felt free to do and be what I wish, and I have felt compelled to analyze endlessly what and who that is. I would like to be able to say it is because I am a thoughtful and analytical person, but this is not true. It is because, in the hard and selfish way in which—usually covertly—the living view the dead, I realized after my mother died I was salvaging one thing from the ruin of my life as I had known it. And that was that I was still alive. I know now that on some unconscious level somewhere in the long and gray months left in that horrid winter, I determined I was going to squeeze every bit of juice from the great gift of a beating heart within my body.

It was only coincidental that, not long after my mother died, I found an unusually safe way to do this. I had wanted to be a writer for most of my life, and in the service of the writing I became a reporter. For many years I was able to observe, even to feel, life vividly, but at secondhand. I was able to stand over the chalk outline of a body on a sidewalk dappled with black blood; to stand behind the glass and look down into an operating theater where one man was placing a heart in the yawning chest of another; to sit in the park on the first day of summer and find myself professionally obligated to record all the glories

of it. Every day I found answers: who, what, when, where, and
why.

But in my own life, as I grew older, I realized I had only
questions. For a long time this made me feel vulnerable and
afraid, and then suddenly, as though I had reached a kind of
emotional puberty, it made me feel vulnerable and comfortable. It is too easy to say that this great change came about when
I had children, although having them, discovering that the
meaning of life is life, trading in the indelible image of my
mother swollen with death for one of myself big as a beach ball
with possibility, certainly contributed to the change. What was
more important was that I finally realized that making sense
of my life meant, in part, accepting the shifting nature of its
sands. My religion changing, one step forward, two steps back;
my marriage always in a state of re-creation and refinement; my
children changing constantly, as children always have: I had
nothing but questions. It was terrifying and fascinating.

One of the most exhilarating parts of it was that my work
became a reflection of my life. After years of being a professional observer of other people's lives, I was given the opportunity to be a professional observer of my own. I was permitted—
and permitted myself—to write a column, not about my
answers, but about my questions. Never did I make so much
sense of my life as I did then, for it was inevitable that as a
writer I would find out most clearly what I thought, and what
I only thought I thought, when I saw it written down. I suddenly knew that at some point in the fifteen years since that
cold winter night, I had come back from the dead. I knew it
because, after years of feeling secondhand, of feeling the pain
of the widow, the joy of the winner, I was able to allow myself
to feel those emotions for myself.

I had often felt alone with these feelings because of the
particular circumstances of my own life. But over the last two

years, as I wrote my columns and read the letters they evoked, I realized more and more that what has happened to me has been typical. A kind of earthquake in the center of my life shook everything up, and left me to rearrange the pieces. Similar earthquakes were felt round the world, precipitated not just by the deaths of people but by the demise of rules, mores, ways of living and thinking. As the aftershocks reverberate, I have had to approach some simple tasks in new ways, and so have the people who have read what I have written. Looking back at my past. Loving my husband. Raising my children. Being a woman. It is no accident that each of those tasks is couched in the present participle, that lovely part of speech that simply goes on and on and on. Oddly enough, what I have learned since that January night many years ago is that life is not so much about beginnings and endings as it is about going on and on and on. It is about muddling through the middle. That is what I am doing now. Muddling through the middle. Living out loud.

LOOKING
BACK

THE
LIGHTNING
BUGS ARE
BACK

he lightning bugs are back. They are small right now, babies really, flying low to the ground as the lawn dissolves from green to black in the dusk. There are constellations of them outside the window: on, off, on, off. At first the little boy cannot see them; then, suddenly, he does. "Mommy, it's magic," he says.

This is why I had children: because of the lightning bugs. Several years ago I was reading a survey in a women's magazine and I tried to answer the questions: Did you decide to have children: A. because of family pressure; B. because it just seemed like the thing to do; C. because of a general liking for children; D. because of religious mandates; E. none of the above.

I looked for the lightning bugs; for the answer that said, because sometime in my life I wanted to stand at a window with a child and show him the lightning bugs and have him say, "Mommy, it's magic." And since nothing even resembling that answer was there, I assumed that, as usual, I was a little twisted, that no one else was so reductive, so obsessed with the telling detail, had a reason so seemingly trivial for a decision so enormous. And then the other night, yellow bug stars flickering around us, my husband said, in a rare moment of perfect unanimity: "That's it. That's why I wanted them, too."

Perhaps we are a reductive species, we human beings. Why else would we so want to distill the slow, often tedious span of our lives to three stiff portraits and a handful of candid shots? The Statue of Liberty is meant to be shorthand for a country so unlike its parts that a trip from California to Indiana should require a passport. In the same way, we all have neat little icons that stand for large, messy lives: a pressed corsage, a wedding dress, a birth announcement, a grade school drawing, a diploma. I look in my high school yearbook and from the picture, the messages, the words that describe me, I can reconstruct four years not unlike the ones little Richie spent in *Happy Days*. Of course, it was completely unlike the years I actually spent at high school. The question is, Do I want to remember it the way it was, or the way it should have been? Did Proust have his cake to inspire his memory or his fantasy?

I know my own answer. The lightning bugs are my madeleine, my cue for a wave of selective recollection. My God, the sensation the other night when the first lightning bug turned his tail on too soon, competing with daylight during the magic hour between dusk and dark. I felt like the anthropologist I once met, who could take a little chunk of femur or a knucklebone and from it describe age, sex, perhaps even height and weight.

From this tiny piece of bone I can reconstruct a childhood: a hot night under tall trees. Squares of lighted windows up and down the dark street. A wiffle ball game in the middle of the road, with the girls and the littlest boys playing the outfield.

The Good-Humor man, in his solid, square truck, the freezer smoky and white when he reaches inside for a Popsicle or a Dixie cup. The dads sitting inside in their Bermuda shorts watching *Car 54, Where Are You?* The moms in the kitchen finishing the dishes. The dull hum of the fans in the bedroom windows. The cheap crack of the wiffle bat. The bells of the ice-cream truck. The lightning bugs trapped in empty peanut-butter jars that have triangular holes in the lids, made with the point of a beer-can opener. The fading smears of phosphores-cent yellow-green, where the older, more jaded kids have used their sneaker soles to smear the lights across the gray pavement. "Let them out," our mothers say, "or they will die in there." Finally, perfect sleep. Sweaty sheets. No dreams.

We were careless. We always forgot to open the jars. The lightning bugs would be there in the morning, their yellow tails dim in the white light of the summer sun, their feet pathetic as they lay on their backs, dead as anything. We were always surprised and a bit horrified by what we had done, or had failed to do. As night fell we shook them out and caught more.

This is why I had children: to offer them a perfect dream of childhood that can fill their souls as they grow older, even as they know that it is only one bone from a sometimes trou-bled body. And to fill my own soul, too, so that I can relive the magic of the yellow light without the bright white of hindsight, to see only the glow and not the dark. Mommy, it's magic, those little flares in the darkness, a distillation of the kind of life we think we had, we wish we had, we want again.

A
PAUL
GIRL

was a Paul girl. Still am, I suppose, at the core.
It was one of four choices you had, in 1964, when
I was on the cusp of adolescence: a Paul girl, a
John girl, a George girl, or a Ringo girl, with all
the attendant Beatle buttons, glossy color pictures, and daydreams. Little did we know that in
some broad way we were defining the sort of
people we were on our way to becoming.

The girls who picked George as their favorite
Beatle were self-contained, serious, with a touch
of the wallflower and a bit of the mystic. The
ones who picked John were aggressive, irreverent,
the smart mouths, the wisecrackers. Ringo got
anyone who was really determined to distinguish
herself, the kind of girl who would wear wax fangs
or weird clothes to get attention, who would
choose the one at the back of the band, with the
big nose and the strange looks. And Paul got the
little ladies like me. He was cute in a mainstream
way, funny in a mainstream way, a public persona

not much different from the most popular boys in the class. He was for girls who were traditional, predictable, who played by the rules.

Who knew what John might do? We Paul girls were not in the least surprised when John blurted out that line about being more popular than Jesus, or when he married Yoko. Paul, on the other hand, was sure to marry a Paul girl and have lots of pretty children, which is precisely what he did. He's even aged wonderfully. Nowadays he looks like one of those computer-generated pictures of someone twenty-five years later, the ones that add only lines and gray hair and overlook the usual accumulation of fat and jowls and rapidly enlarging forehead.

Over the years I've sometimes tried to escape being a Paul girl, but it's never worked for long. I once made an attempt in high school, taking a crack at a hefty blonde who'd made fun of me in the cafeteria and missing her substantial jaw by a good six inches because of bad eye-hand coordination. And once or twice, particularly in convent school, I've had friends so good-natured and conformist that they made me seem like Irma La Douce for a time. When the going got tough, however, I always wound up a Paul girl again. I'd had lots of practice. One of the most satisfying things about growing up Catholic during the 1950s were the rules, which were not then, as we say now, flexible. The only questions were of degree: If you inadvertently ate baloney at lunch on Friday, would you go to hell if you were hit by a car during recess afterward? If you sucked on a cough drop in the car on the way to nine o'clock mass, had you violated the Communion fast requirements? And which was worse: to leave a piece of Host stuck to the roof of your mouth during breakfast, or to move it with your finger in direct violation of what the nuns had told you about stuck Hosts?

Is it any wonder I became accustomed to the letter of the law? Rules were a relief. They were like basic tap-dance combinations: you could set them up any way you pleased, add the stray shuffle or heel-and-toe, but at least you didn't have to improvise everything. Of course there were always the people who seemed not to need rules—the John girls, as it were. My last year in high school I nursed a secret admiration for them, even while I scrambled each morning to match kilt and crew neck, circle pin and earrings, knee socks and Weejuns. In Indian-print dresses and sandals, the John girls skipped pep rallies, asked the history teacher whether Richard Nixon wasn't as bad as Adolf Hitler, and applied to alternative schools.

I got to know them better in college, and realized that they had their own set of rules, and that they distrusted deviation and liked conformity as much as I did. Talk about how high you got even if you didn't; look bored; disdain all academic disciplines except for philosophy and creative writing; use rhyme in poetry only on pain of death; and affect a writing style as close as possible to that of *Franny and Zooey*. That was how their game was played.

We've all changed a good bit since then, although when I wear dinner-plate earrings just because everyone else is wearing dinner-plate earrings, I sometimes have my doubts. More of my life now is about character building than image making. While there aren't quite as many rules as there once were (you can pull a piece of baloney out of your purse in church on Friday and nobody seems to mind as long as you show up) I distrust them more. They just don't work as well for human relationships as we might like. I wouldn't insult either my husband or myself by reading one of those one-minute marriage manager books. And as far as kids are concerned, the rules are just plain silly, as you find out the first time you try to give a baby his every-four-hour nurse and discover that an hour-and-a-half later he's hungry again.

I guess I can tap-dance better now—more improvising, fewer set pieces. I think of the Paul girl as a bit like an illustration in a coloring book: black outlines, no fill-in. It was useful in its time, in its place. It made it easier to believe in God, to hate certain people passionately, to choose Paul without thinking twice about any of the other three. Of course, I now understand the bits of those three that were attractive to others; I understand the gestalt, which was a concept, not to mention a word, that was beyond me at the time.

I saw Paul on television the other day. He seemed to have changed less than I had. He doesn't appeal to me as much anymore; neither does the safety he once personified.

AT THE BEACH

The lifeguard's girlfriend is blonde. Hasn't it always been so? Her tan is the color of Karo syrup. Her shoulders are broader than her hips. And when she swims, her head knifes perfectly through each wave, so that she emerges sleek and shiny, a golden seal.

Here we are in the land that time forgot. It has been nearly twenty years since I last spent the summer in this seashore town. There is bad modern architecture where once there were dunes, but nothing else really has changed, except for me. On Sunday mornings the same people hold the same numbers in Jack's Bakery; the same white wooden boats lie waiting for disaster to one side of the same white wooden lifeguard stands. And the sea, arrogant as always, rises, falls and breaks, rises, falls and breaks, silver green to the horizon. Its message is clear: "You grew up, you went away," it says. "You married, had children, came back. Who cares? Who cares?"

I did not know it would be like this, although perhaps I should have. Life here was never what I expected. I grew up here, not just because the time passed, but because the time I passed was some of the loneliest of my life. I never understood why we did it, pulled up all our roots each June to journey to a succession of rented Cape Cod-style cottages, with not a decent knife or spaghetti pot in a one of them, to rest and relax among strangers.

My mother neither drove nor swam; despite her olive complexion she burned, and her prominent nose was a terrible shade of red all summer long. There was too much laundry and too little hot water. My fantasies of an endless summer always ended badly. I went to dances at the local firehouse, with a consuming need shining so brightly from my light eyes in my tanned face that only the boldest or blindest asked me to dance. Mostly I read and walked for miles at night along the beach, writing bad blank verse and searching endlessly for someone wonderful who would step out of the darkness and change my life. It never crossed my mind that that person could be me.

This was called the vacation. It still is, and is still, in some ways, inexplicable. The first day here, as night began to fall, my elder son said, "We go home now, Mommy." He was appalled to find that I expected him to sleep in this strange place. And beneath the hard eye of the sun, next to the smug sea, the loneliness once again grabbed me by the throat. It had a new weapon this time. A girl who once cultivated a tan and tried ineptly to pick up boys, I was now too old to do either. The lifeguard's girlfriend is young enough to be my daughter. "Who cares," the water said. "Who cares?"

It is still a puzzle to me why we do this, although it becomes a little clearer every day. Amid the muddle of strange beds and new habits and sand in the sheets, a moment will blaze through: the hieroglyphics of gulls' tracks in the salt-and-pepper sand, the long climb up the lighthouse steps, the sand crabs in the green plastic bucket, dug up every fifteen minutes or so to make sure they are still there. That is why we are here: so that our children can have these moments, or so that we can watch them have them. I do not know which.

I am here to look for someone. She might just be me—a younger me, a different me. There is something about this place that makes me aware of the Russian-doll aspect of personality, the little round papier-mâché woman in the babushka inside another, and another, and another, the child inside the girl inside the woman.

Once, when I was in my early teens, I became intrigued by a theory that time was really place, that all history is taking place in some other location. It is a profoundly dumb theory (and horrifying when applied to waiting in bank lines), but sometimes here I almost believe it. I expect to come around the right corner, past the right telephone booth, and see a vaguely familiar sixteen-year-old waiting for a call from some moron with a nice car and a letter in wrestling. What a horrible thought—the thirty-four-year-old me trying to convince her of the monumental waste of time, the sixteen-year-old me wondering why this lady with the two kids and the gray in her bangs is haranguing her. If I was so vulnerable and stupid then, can I really be so strong and smart now?

I was not surprised when the deep-sea pictures of the *Titanic* showed it perfectly preserved, down to the crystal chandeliers. It has happened here. Fifty years from now, if I am lucky, I will be an old lady in a rubber beach chair, staring at the water, seeing them all, all the little papier-mâché people: the little girl with the T-shirt over her bathing suit, the teenager listening to the radio and glistening with baby oil, the mother of babies, the mother of teenagers, the grandmother. "Who cares?" the water will whisper, but by then it will have lost its awful power over me, and I will no longer hear it.

REUNION

R obert called me "baby" just recently. "Same old Robert," Donna said. The only difference was that the last time he said it I was thirteen years old and unsure whether I was supposed to be amused, offended, or flattered. He was my best boyfriend, with the emphasis on the *friend*. We spent hours on the phone together each night deciding which girl deserved his tie clip. I still know the telephone number at his mother's house by heart.

I went to the twentieth reunion of my eighth grade class the other night. It was nearly a five-hour drive, there and back. Some people I know thought I was a little crazy: high school, maybe, or college, but grade school? Perhaps they went to a different kind of school.

A couple of dozen of us started out together when we were small children, and stayed together until we were just entering adolescence. Those were the people with whom I learned the alphabet and the Our Father, how to shoot from the foul line and do a cartwheel. Those were some of the most important years of my life. We know now how important the early years are, but the early years lasted longer then, and while the bedrock on which I am built came from my family, many of my first lessons in friendship, loss, loyalty, and love came from a group of people I have not seen for two decades. They have always seemed somehow more real to me than most of the people I have known since.

It was odd, how much the same we all looked. It would have been hard for the women to look worse, or at least worse than our graduation picture, with all of us grouped on the lawn by the convent. Most of us look younger now than we did there, our poor hair lacquered into beehives or baloney curls, our feet squeezed into pumps with pointed toes.

And it was odd how much the same we were, odd how early the raw material had been set. Robert was still the class flirt, Janet still elegant. "Refined" was how I described her in a sixth-grade composition—a funny word for an eleven-year-old girl, and yet the right one, particularly now that it suited her so. In the photograph, Alicia and Susie are sitting together; they drove down together, arrived together, were still friends. In the photograph, Donna and I are next to each other, trying not to crack up. "Still inseparable," said Jeff, the class president, looking down at the two of us giggling on the steps. The truth was that although we had not met for fifteen years, the ice was broken within minutes.

I'm not sure that I would have done well at a tenth reunion. If the raw material is laid down in those first thirteen years, the next thirteen sometimes seem to me to have been given over fruitlessly to the art of artifice, the attempt to hide the flaws beneath a construction as false as those 1966 beehives. Now I am much more who I am, with fewer regrets, apologies, and attempts to be something else. To be honest, I am much more

like 1966 than I would have been likely to admit ten years ago.
Perhaps it was the beer, but some of the others seemed to be
letting down their defenses, too.

Ed remembered that when he had had to think of his most
embarrassing moment for a Dale Carnegie course, it was something that had happened in elementary school. ("You're not
going to put it in?" he asked plaintively, a lifetime after it
happened, and so I said I would not.) And Jim, the host of the
party, suddenly said as he saw Robert and me trading wise-
cracks, "You guys and your clique," making me think, for the
first time, really of how thoughtlessly hurtful we were then, too.
I suppose in a way it was like many reunions. We talked about
the time we Crazy-Foamed the gym, went on class picnics to
Naylor's Run and dared to go to the public-school canteen.
There were children to discuss, and deaths and divorces. Most
of the men still lived in the area. Most of the women had
moved away. Most of the men came with their wives. Most of
the women came alone.

And yet I felt that it was a different kind of occasion, at least
for me. Steve had brought photographs from class trips and
parties, and in one of them there I was in the front in a plaid
dress, my bangs cut too short, my new front teeth a little too
big for my face, and it was like looking at one of those photographs of an embryo. On Jim's back porch I looked around and
I saw so many prototypes: my first close friendship, my first
jealousies, my first boyfriend—all the things that break you in
for all the things that are yet to come. I felt like Emily in *Our
Town*.

Robert and I talked a lot about Martha. It turned out that
over the years he had never forgotten her. He was crushed that
she had not been able to come up from Florida where she is
a teacher. Besides, he said, she still has his tie clip. But it wasn't
really Martha he was talking about as much as a basic model
he learned then. He liked her and she liked him. It was only

later that he, I, and all the rest of us learned that is the basic model, but it sometimes it comes with fins and a sunroof, with games and insecurities and baggage that are just barely burgeoning when you are thirteen years old.

On the stereo was a song, a 45, that we must have played thousands of times in my living room: "She Loves You" by the Beatles. "With a love like that, you know you should be glad." Robert played the drums. I sang. He made a grab for me, and I slipped past him. "Same old Robert," I said to Donna.

CATS

The cats came with the house. They lived in the backyards, tiger gray, orange marmalade, calico, black. They slithered through the evergreens at the back perimeter, and during mating season their screams were terrible. Sometimes I shook black pepper along the property line, and for a night or two all was still. Then the rain came and they were back.

The cats came because of the woman next door. She and her husband, said to be bedridden, had lived on the third floor for many years. Every evening after dinner she went into the alley with a foil pie plate heaped with cat food and scraps: cabbage, rice, the noodles from chicken noodle soup, whatever they had had for dinner. Before she would even get to the bottom of the stairs the cats would begin to assemble, narrowing their eyes. She would talk to them roughly in a voice like sandpaper, coarse from years of cigarette smoke. "Damn cats," she grumbled as she bent to put the food down.

She had only two interests besides the cats: my son and her own. She and her husband had one grown child. I never heard her say a bad word about him. He had reportedly walked and talked early, been as beautiful as a child star, never given a bit of trouble. He always sent a large card on Mother's Day, and each Christmas a poinsettia came, wrapped in green foil with a red bow. He was in the military, stationed here and there. During the time we lived next door to her, he came home once. She said it broke his heart not to see his father more. She said they had always been close when he lived at home, that he played baseball for the high school team and that his father never missed a game. He was a crack shortstop, she said, and a superior hitter.

She called my son "Bop Bop" because of the way he bounced in my arms. It was one of the first things he learned to say, and when he was in the backyard on summer evenings he would call "Bop Bop" plaintively until she came to her apartment window. As she raised the screen the cats would begin to mass in a great Pavlovian gesture at the head of the alley. "Are you being a good boy?" she would call down. Bop Bop would smile up, his eyes shining. "Cat," he said, pointing, and the cats looked, too. Some summer nights she and my little boy would sit together companionably on the front stoop, watching the cars go by. She did not talk to him very much, and she wasn't tender, but when he was very good and not terribly dirty she sometimes said he looked just like her own little boy, only his hair wasn't quite as thick.

Last year she fell on the street and broke her hip, but while she was in the hospital, they found that she had fallen because she had had a stroke, and she had had a stroke because of brain cancer. I went to see her in the hospital, and brought a picture of my son. She propped it against the water pitcher. She asked me to take care of her parakeet until she came home, to look in on her husband and to feed the cats. At night, when I came back from work, they would be prowling the yards, crying pitifully. My dogs lunged at the back windows.

When the ambulance brought her home, she looked like a scarecrow, her arms broomsticks in the armholes of her housecoat, her white hair wild. A home health-care aide came and cared for her and her husband. The woman across the street told me she was not well enough to take the bird back. The cats climbed the fire escape and banged against the screens with their bullet heads, but the aide shooed them away. My son would stand in the backyard and call "Bop Bop" at the window. One evening she threw it open and leaned out, a death's head, and shouted at him, and he cried. "Bop Bop is very sick," I said, and gave him a Popsicle.

She died this winter, a month after her husband. Her son came home for the funerals with his wife, and together they cleaned out the apartment. We sent roses to the funeral home, and the son's wife sent a nice thank-you note. The bird died the next month. Slowly the cats began to disperse. The two biggest, a tom and a female, seem to have stayed. I don't really feed them, but sometimes my son will eat lunch out back; if he doesn't finish his food, I will leave it on the table. When I look out again it is gone, and the dogs are a little wild.

My son likes to look through photo albums. In one there is a picture of her leaning out the window, and a picture of him looking up with a self-conscious smile. He calls them both "Bop Bop." I wonder for how long he will remember, and what it will mean to him, years from now, when he looks at the picture and sees her at her window, what reverberations will begin, what lasting lessons will she have subliminally taught him, what lasting lessons will she not so subliminally have taught me.

BOOKWORM

came late to the down comforter. I thought it was a fad. Ducks have never looked particularly warm and cozy to me, and two hundred dollars seems like an awful lot to pay for a blanket. Now I admit I was wrong. Even on summer nights I lie beneath its featherweight and feel secure. Over the intercom on the table just next to my left ear, I imagine I can hear the sounds of the children snuffling softly in the rooms on the floor above. There is pink fiber-glass insulation in my crawl space and an infrared light illuminating the backyard with a bulb the electrician says may last my lifetime, if I don't live too long. And downstairs my bookshelves are filled with books.

Strange things make me feel secure. I can't honestly say how much money is in the savings account, and I still think of an I.R.A. as some black hole that I throw $2,000 into each year, like the mouth of some big carnivore at the zoo. But

I couldn't get along without the cream pitcher shaped like a cat that my mother got as a shower gift, or the omelet pan that my Aunt Catherine gave me when I graduated from high school, or my books.

I moved a fair amount when I was a kid. I wasn't exactly an army brat, but I didn't even come close to being married in the house where we lived when I was born. So I have a tendency to assemble all these talismans, wrap them in newspaper, and take them from place to place. The books were always most important because they were not simply objects, but portable friends. Sometimes at night I lie in the dark beneath my insulated crawl space and these words come to mind: "It is a truth universally acknowledged, that a single man in possession of a good fortune must be in want of a wife." It is the first sentence of *Pride and Prejudice*. It is the only sentence in any book in the English language I know perfectly by heart, except for the beginning of the Gospel of John, the part about, "In the beginning was the Word."

Pride and Prejudice is not really my favorite book, although it is definitely in the top ten, along with *Bleak House, The Sound and the Fury, Sons and Lovers, Anna Karenina, Gone With the Wind* and a series about two girls in Minnesota called the Betsy-Tacy books. But it is the book that makes me most feel that everything is going to be all right, that the world is a hospitable place and that, as Anne Frank once said, people are really good at heart.

Why it should do this when it was published in 1813 and those feelings in the late twentieth century are so patently untrue, I do not know. Part of it is that *Pride and Prejudice* has been with me for a long time, since I was twelve. Part is that it is about a young woman named Elizabeth Bennet, who I have always felt would have been my best friend if she hadn't been fictional. Part is that it is about the right things happen-

ing in the wrong way—chance meetings leading to rapproche-
ments, misunderstandings leading to marriages—in just the
way you wish would happen in real life.

Most important, I feel at home in this book. There is a great
short story by Woody Allen called "The Kugelmass Episode,"
in which a college professor arranges for a conjurer to let him
become a character in *Madame Bovary* and have a love affair
with her. All over the world Flaubert scholars start wondering
about this guy Kugelmass on page 94. I feel that I could just
slip unnoticed into *Pride and Prejudice*. Elizabeth and I could
sit around jawboning about what a pain Mr. Darcy is, while all
the time I'd be secretly thinking he is just the guy for her.

I never tire of Elizabeth Bennet or her family, even her silly
mother. One summer my family moved to West Virginia—
and, believe me, I was not West Virginia material. The Ben-
nets saved my life. They moved with me, and I spent all my
time with them until, finally, I made some friends. The only
thing I don't like about *Pride and Prejudice* is the ending,
because then it's over.

I don't feel this way about anything written much after
1940. I've always liked to hang around bookstores; among other
things, I like the way they smell. But nowadays I stand in front
of the fiction shelves and feel like a stranger in a strange land.
I picture myself showing up in one of these books in which
people sit around their kitchens and talk to their cats about
what they bought at Bloomingdale's, and I figure readers would
just think, "Who's that weird woman sitting over in the corner
with the paperback copy of *Pride and Prejudice*, looking so
sad?" I feel much the same way about objects, too, which is
why I seem to buy so many antiques, even though they're uncomfortable and often appear to have no function whatsoever.

Maybe I just haven't given the modern enough time to make
me feel at home. Maybe twenty years from now I'll look at a
Dansk vase on a shelf, and it will make me feel warm all over.

Maybe there will be some new hip modern novel that will take me in its arms and make me part of it, give me a new best friend and a first sentence that will make me feel as good in the middle of the night as the sound of the person in the room above me turning over in his crib. After all, I came late to down comforters. In the meantime, Elizabeth and I are really worried about her sister Jane. She's stuck on this guy named Bingley and things don't look good. But trust me, we'll work it all out in the end.

HALLOWEEN

When I was a little girl, I loved Halloween because it was the only day of the year when I was beautiful. I had friends who went out dressed as hobos and clowns and witches, but I never would. I was always a princess or a ballet dancer, Sleeping Beauty or Cinderella. (One year I wanted to go as Barbie. "Out of the question," said my mother flatly, and it occurs to me now that her reply worked on several levels.)

It was the only day of the year when I wore satin or net or hoops, the only day of the year when my thin lips were carmine and full and the mole on my upper lip, blackened with eyebrow pencil, became a beauty mark. I remember one Halloween, when I wore my cousin Mary Jane's flower-girl dress, blue net over blue chiffon over blue satin, with a skirt as big around at the bottom as a hula hoop, as one of the happiest nights of my life. I had a wand with a silver star on the end made of tinfoil, and a tiara that was borrowed from a girl down the street who was last year's prom princess. My hair had been set in pin curls, and waves rose all over my head like a cross between Shirley Temple and Elsa Lanchester in *Bride of Frankenstein*. I looked in the mirror on the back of my closet door and saw someone I was not, and loved her. The night was sharp, as perfect Halloween nights always are, but I would not wear a coat. I caught cold, and didn't care.

I suppose one of the things that makes me saddest about modern life, right up there with the fact that most of the furniture is so cheesy, is that Halloween has fallen into some disrepute. The candy is not good for you. The store-bought costumes stink. And behind every door a mother is supposed to imagine that there's a man with candied apples whose recipe for caramelization includes rat poison. My children don't go far on Halloween, at least in part because they are city kids. They visit a few neighbors, get just enough stuff to make a kind of promising rustle in the bottom of their bags. They are amazed at even this much license; the rest of the year they live with a woman whose idea of a good time is a bag of yogurt raisins. They must think I've lost it when I stand before the jack-o'-lantern at the kitchen table, grinning maniacally at one of those miniature Mr. Goodbars. I have never in my life eaten a Mr. Goodbar, except in the aftermath of Halloween.

In the way they do—must, I suppose—my children are galvanized by Halloween because I am, just as they make a big fuss about throwing autumn leaves up in the air and letting them tumble over their heads. They take their cue from me. The little one is still a bit confused, but the elder caught fire last year. "I want to be a clown," he said. And even though, throughout the month, he ricocheted between wanting to be a bumblebee and a bunny, he always inevitably came back to wanting to be a clown. His cheeks were painted with red circles, the tip of his nose was blue, and although he was sick for four days beforehand he insisted on dragging himself around to a half-dozen houses in his satin clown costume with the pompons and the big ruffle around his reedy neck. A sensitive, thoughtful little boy, who loves to laugh but never likes to feel laughed at, he looked in the mirror and saw some-one he was not. "I look really great," he said.

(By contrast, the little one was a bunny, quite himself in artificial white pile. "Hop, hop, hop," he said for three hours. "Hop, hop, hop," he said for two weeks afterward. Of course, I chose the costume, and when he chooses for himself perhaps he will choose something more contrary to his essential nature. Like a clerical collar. This year he is a black cat, which is just right.)

This year the elder boy is a witch, which is just right, too. He says he loves witches because they are mean and nasty, although he is not mean and nasty at all. He will wear a black robe, a pointed hat, and wrinkles made of eyeliner. A broom but no wig. "I am a boy witch," he says with dignity.

I, of course, go along for the ride, at least for the next few years, until the day when they say "Mo-om!" in that unpleas-ant, whiny voice and march off by themselves with their pillow-cases, their voices muffled behind their masks. Last year I thought seriously about dressing up as something for the sake of verisimilitude—I'm short, I could pass!—but abandoned the idea in a rare moment of complete and total common sense. This year I will not be so foolish.

The other day on the telephone a friend recalled one of the saddest moments of her youth: the night when her sister came home in tears and announced that she had become too old to go out on Halloween. I remember it, too—that night looking into the mirror at a Gypsy, with hoop earrings and a rakish headscarf and an off-the-shoulder peasant blouse, and knowing in a kind of clear, horrible grown-up way that it was something I was not. And getting door duty from then on in, giving out

M & M's to kids who were rowdy, jubilant, somehow freed from themselves, and happy not to find behind the door one of those moms who gave out apples. I've been on door duty every Halloween since. Last year I suppose I wanted to make one last stab at the magic. But the wand's been passed.

BEING

A

WOMAN

WOMEN
ARE JUST
BETTER

y favorite news story so far this year was the one
saying that in England scientists are working on
a way to allow men to have babies. I'd buy tickets
to that. I'd be happy to stand next to any man I
know in one of those labor rooms the size of a
Volkswagen trunk and whisper "No, dear, you
don't really need the Demerol; just relax and do
your second-stage breathing." It puts me in mind
of an old angry feminist slogan: "If men got pregnant, abortion would be a sacrament." I think
this is specious. If men got pregnant, there would
be safe, reliable methods of birth control. They'd
be inexpensive, too.

I can almost hear some of you out there thinking that I do not like men. This isn't true. I have
been married for some years to a man and I hope
that someday our two sons will grow up to be
men. All three of my brothers are men, as is my
father. Some of my best friends are men. It is
simply that I think women are superior to men.

There, I've said it. It is my dirty little secret. We're not supposed to say it because in the old days men used to say that women were superior. What they meant was that we were too wonderful to enter courtrooms, enjoy sex, or worry our minds about money. Obviously, this is not what I mean at all.

The other day a very wise friend of mine asked: "Have you ever noticed that what passes as a terrific man would only be an adequate woman?" A Roman candle went off in my head; she was absolutely right. What I expect from my male friends is that they are polite and clean. What I expect from my female friends is unconditional love, the ability to finish my sentences for me when I am sobbing, a complete and total willingness to pour their hearts out to me, and the ability to tell me why the meat thermometer isn't supposed to touch the bone.

The inherent superiority of women came to mind just the other day when I was reading about sanitation workers. New York City has finally hired women to pick up the garbage, which makes sense to me, since, as I've discovered, a good bit of being a woman consists of picking up garbage. There was a story about the hiring of these female sanitation workers, and I was struck by the fact that I could have written that story without ever leaving my living room—a reflection not upon the quality of the reporting but the predictability of the male sanitation workers' responses.

The story started by describing the event, and then the two women, who were just your average working women trying to make a buck and get by. There was something about all the maneuvering that had to take place before they could be hired, and then there were the obligatory quotes from male sanitation workers about how women were incapable of doing the job. They were similar to quotes I have read over the years suggesting that women are not fit to be rabbis, combat soldiers, astronauts, firefighters, judges, ironworkers, and President of the United States. Chief among them was a comment from one sanitation worker, who said it just wasn't our kind of job, that women were cut out to do dishes and men were cut out to do yard work.

As a woman who has done dishes, yard work, and tossed a fair number of Hefty bags, I was peeved—more so because I would fight for the right of any laid-off sanitation man to work, for example, at the gift-wrap counter at Macy's, even though any woman knows that men are hormonally incapable of wrapping packages or tying bows.

I simply can't think of any jobs any more that women can't do. Come to think of it, I can't think of any job women don't do. I know lots of men who are full-time lawyers, doctors, editors and the like. And I know lots of women who are full-time lawyers and part-time interior decorators, pastry chefs, algebra teachers, and garbage slingers. Women are the glue that holds our day-to-day world together.

Maybe the sanitation workers who talk about the sex division of duties are talking about girls just like the girls that married dear old dad. Their day is done. Now lots of women know that if they don't carry the garbage bag to the curb, it's not going to get carried—either because they're single, or their husband is working a second job, or he's staying at the office until midnight, or he just left them.

I keep hearing that there's a new breed of men out there who don't talk about helping a woman as though they're doing you a favor and who do seriously consider leaving the office if a child comes down with a fever at school, rather than assuming that you will leave yours. But from what I've seen, there aren't enough of these men to qualify as a breed, only as a subgroup.

This all sounds angry; it is. After a lifetime spent with winds of sexual change buffeting me this way and that, it still makes me angry to read the same dumb quotes with the same dumb stereotypes that I was reading when I was eighteen. It makes me angry to realize that after so much change, very little is different. It makes me angry to think that these two female sanitation workers will spend their days doing a job most of their co-workers think they can't handle, and then they will go home and do another job most of their co-workers don't want.

THE
JANE

 ne day I was standing in a bathroom in City Hall washing my hands when the city council president stepped up to the sink beside me. (I will stop here, lest I precipitate another city scandal, to say that at the time the city council president was a woman.) We began to chat, and eventually our chat turned to matters of moment, and eventually the matters of moment became newsworthy. I left the bathroom with a story. After years of worrying that the best stories were coming out of conversations in the men's room, I also left with the conviction that journalism was going to be all right for women after all.

My mind goes back to that day when I think of what I consider the worst scare tactic employed by people opposed to the proposed equal rights amendment. This was the suggestion that passage of the measure would lead to unisex bathrooms. (Nearly as objectionable was the use of the word "unisex," which should by law be applied only to certain hair salons to let you know that they are the kind of places you want to avoid.) I can assure everyone that if a piece of legislation took away restricted access to the jane—as I prefer to call the female john—I would march in the streets to protest its passage.

Little has been written about the role of the jane in the life of the contemporary career woman. It is impossible to overestimate its importance. In some ways it has replaced the old consciousness-raising group as a setting for the free exchange of ideas about men, work, children, personal development, and the ridiculous price of pantyhose. In most offices, it is one of the few spots in which a woman employee can pause, throw back her head, and say, loudly, "Men are so stupid sometimes I want to shoot all of them." The only difficulty is that this statement often precipitates a free exchange of ideas for a full half hour.

I have also frequently used the jane—I'm not ashamed to say it—to apply makeup. Recently I read an etiquette question about whether it is permissible to apply makeup at your desk. The answer was no, that it was in bad taste. The answer should have been, no, not if you ever want to be taken seriously again. I actually came closer to having a baby at my desk than I ever did to applying makeup there. (An extenuating circumstance was that several of my male coworkers thought that I never wore makeup, which was a testimonial either to the deftness of the application or the futility of the effort.) In the jane you can get right down to business and unload your purse: blush, blush brush, lipstick, concealer, mascara, hair brush. Apply blush, apply lipstick, use concealer under eyes, touch up mascara, bend at the waist, drop head, brush hair, throw head and mane back, check out the results. Show me a woman who would do this in her office and I'll show you a woman who will never get promoted.

I have also cried in the jane. This is a major admission.

During my early years in the newspaper business in New York, there was a young woman of about my age who became famous for having burst into tears—in the middle of the office—when criticized by an editor. (To be fair, the editor reportedly pointed to the first paragraph of her story and said, "What the hell is this supposed to mean?" in a voice that carried beyond the newspaper circulation area.) At the time, those of us who were the same generation and gender as our unfortunate colleague vowed that no one would ever see our tears in the office.

Perhaps for some of my colleagues this pledge meant they would never cry. For me, however, it meant occasionally going to the jane, locking myself in a stall and sobbing while I flushed the toilet repeatedly so that no one could hear me. I would then emerge with a complexion as mottled as Genoa salami, make a few remarks about something stuck under my contact lens (I do not wear contact lenses), and then take out the blush, the blush brush, the lipstick, and the rest and wash and remake my face while everyone in the jane tactfully looked away or pretended to be talking about sexual harassment, the latest Supreme Court decision, or the white sale at Bloomingdale's. I would emerge from the jane looking as if nothing had happened.

I shouldn't suggest that there are no bad things about the jane, because there are. One of the most unforgettable bad moments of my life took place in one, my last year in high school. I entered and the room fell silent, so silent you could hear the water running through the pipes. There was only one explanation; everyone had been talking about me. To this day I can remember the color of the wall tiles. They were beige.

But at the same time, some of the fastest friendships I have ever made were made in the jane. There is something about washing your hands side-by-side with another human being that breaks down socially learned barriers of reserve. (This explains why surgeons are so friendly with other surgeons, sometimes to the exclusion of everyone else.) I met many of my female friends by swapping exasperations with them in the jane: "What a day!" "I've had it with this place!" "If he gives me a hard time one more time!" and the like. Some of them were even people who had seen me cry, although they would never say anything, except maybe, "Need a tissue?"

I think any of those people could tell you that if the proposed equal rights amendment was likely to turn the jane and the john into some androgynous hybrid called the jackie, I would be one of the first to stand up and say, "Enough!"

THE NAME IS MINE

am on the telephone to the emergency room of the local hospital. My elder son is getting stitches in his palm, and I have called to make myself feel better, because I am at home, waiting, and my husband is there, holding him. I am thirty-four years old, and I am crying like a child, making a slippery mess of my face. "Mrs. Krovatin?" says the nurse, and for the first time in my life I answer "Yes."

This is a story about a name. The name is mine. I was given it at birth, and I have never changed it, although I married. I could come up with lots of reasons why. It was a political decision, a simple statement that I was somebody and not an adjunct of anybody, especially a husband. As a friend of mine told her horrified mother, "He didn't adopt me, he married me." It was a professional and a personal decision, too. I grew up with an ugly dog of a name, one I came to love because I though it was weird and unlovable.

Amid the Debbies and Kathys of my childhood, I had a first name only grandmothers had and a last name that began with a strange letter. "Sorry, the letters I, O, Q, U, V, X, Y, and Z are not available," the catalogues said about monogrammed key rings and cocktail napkins. Seeing my name in black on white at the top of a good story, suddenly it wasn't an ugly dog anymore.

But neither of these are honest reasons, because they assume rational consideration, and it so happens that when it came to changing my name, there was no consideration, rational or otherwise. It was mine. It belonged to me. I don't even share a checking account with my husband. Damned if I was going to be hidden beneath the umbrella of his identity. It seemed like a simple decision. But nowadays I think the only simple decisions are whether to have grilled cheese or tuna fish for lunch. Last week, my older child wanted an explanation of why he, his dad, and his brother have one name and I have another.

My answer was long, philosophical, and rambling—that is to say, unsatisfactory. What's in a name? I could have said disingenuously. But I was talking to a person who had just spent three torturous, exhilarating years learning names for things, and I wanted to communicate to him that mine meant something quite special to me, had seemed as form-fitting as my skin, and as painful to remove. Personal identity and independence, however, were not what he was looking for; he just wanted to make sure I was one of them. And I am—and then again, I am not. When I made this decision, I was part of a couple. Now, there are two of me, the me who is the individual and the me who is part of a family of four, a family of four in which, in a small way, I am left out.

A wise friend who finds herself in the same fix says she never wants to change her name, only to have a slightly different identity as a family member, an identity for pediatricians' offices and parent-teacher conferences. She also says that the entire situation reminds her of the women's movement as a whole. We did these things as individuals, made these decisions about ourselves and what we wanted to be and do. And they were good decisions, the right decisions. But we based them on individual choice, not on group dynamics. We thought in terms of our sense of ourselves, not our relationships with others.

Some people found alternative solutions: hyphenated names, merged names, matriarchal names for the girls and patriarchal ones for the boys, one name at work and another at home. I did not like those choices; I thought they were middle grounds, and I didn't live much in the middle ground at the time. I was once slightly disdainful of women who went all the way and changed their names. But I now know too many smart, independent, terrific women who have the same last names as their husbands to be disdainful anymore. (Besides, if I made this decision as part of a feminist world view, it seems dishonest to turn around and trash other women for deciding as they did.)

I made my choice. I haven't changed my mind. I've just changed my life. Sometimes I feel like one of those worms I used to hear about in biology, the ones that, snipped in half, walked off in different directions. My name works fine for one half, not quite as well for the other. I would never give it up. Except for that one morning when I talked to the nurse at the hospital, I always answer the question "Mrs. Krovatin?" with "No, this is Mr. Krovatin's wife." It's just that I understand the down side now.

When I decided not to disappear beneath my husband's umbrella, it did not occur to me that I would be the only one left outside. It did not occur to me that I would ever care—not enough to change, just enough to think about the things we do on our own and what they mean when we aren't on our own anymore.

PREGNANT
IN
NEW YORK

have two enduring memories of the hours just
before I gave birth to my first child. One is of
finding a legal parking space on Seventy-eighth
Street between Lexington and Park, which made
my husband and me believe that we were going
inside the hospital to have a child who would
always lead a charmed life. The other is of walking down Lexington Avenue, stopping every couple of steps to find myself a visual focal point—a
stop sign, a red light, a pair of $200 shoes in a
store window—and doing what the Lamaze
books call first-stage breathing. It was 3:00 A.M.
and coming toward me through a magenta haze
of what the Lamaze books call discomfort were
a couple in evening clothes whose eyes were pop-
ping out of their perfect faces. "Wow," said the
man when I was at least two steps past them.
"She looks like she's ready to burst."

I love New York, but it's a tough place to be
pregnant. It's a great place for half sour pickles,

chopped liver, millionaires, actors, dancers, akita dogs, nice leather goods, fur coats, and baseball, but it is a difficult place to have any kind of disability and, as anyone who has filled out the forms for a maternity leave lately will tell you, pregnancy is considered a disability. There's no privacy in New York; everyone is right up against everyone else and they all feel compelled to say what they think. When you look like a hot-air balloon with insufficient ballast, that's not good.

New York has no pity: it's every man for himself, and since you are yourself-and-a-half, you fall behind. There's a rumor afoot that if you are pregnant you can get a seat on the A train at rush hour, but it's totally false. There are, in fact, parts of the world in which pregnancy can get you a seat on public transportation, but none of them are within the boundaries of the city—with the possible exception of some unreconstructed parts of Staten Island.

What you get instead are rude comments, unwarranted intrusions and deli countermen. It is a little-known fact that New York deli countermen can predict the sex of an unborn child. (This is providing that you order, of course. For a counterman to provide this service requires a minimum order of seventy-five cents.) This is how it works: You walk into a deli and say, "Large fruit salad, turkey on rye with Russian, a large Perrier and a tea with lemon." The deli counterman says, "Who you buying for, the Rangers?" and all the other deli countermen laugh.

This is where many pregnant women make their mistake. If it is wintertime and you are wearing a loose coat, the preferred answer to this question is, "I'm buying for all the women in my office." If it is summer and you are visibly pregnant, you are sunk. The deli counterman will lean over the counter and say, studying your contours, "It's a boy." He will then tell a tedious story about sex determination, his Aunt Olga, and a clove of garlic, while behind you people waiting on line shift and sigh and begin to make Zero Population Growth and fat people comments. (I once dealt with an East Side counterman who argued with me about the tea because he said it was bad for the baby, but he was an actor waiting for his big break, not a professional.) Deli countermen do not believe in amniocentesis. Friends who have had amniocentesis tell me that once or twice they tried to argue: "I already know it's a girl." "You are wrong." They gave up: "Don't forget the napkins."

There are also cabdrivers. One promptly pulled over in the middle of Central Park when I told him I had that queasy feeling. When I turned to get back into the cab, it was gone. The driver had taken the $1.80 on the meter as a loss. Luckily, I never had this problem again, because as I grew larger, nine out of ten cabdrivers refused to pick me up. They had read the tabloids. They knew about all those babies christened Checker (actually, I suppose now most of them are Plymouths) because they're born in the back seat in the Midtown Tunnel. The only way I could get a cabdriver to pick me up after the sixth month was to hide my stomach by having a friend walk in front of me. The exception was a really tiresome young cabdriver whose wife's due date was a week after mine and who wanted to practice panting with me for that evening's childbirth class. Most of the time I wound up taking public transportation.

And so it came down to the subways: men looking at their feet, reading their newspapers, working hard to keep from noticing me. One day on the IRT I was sitting down—it was a spot left unoccupied because the rainwater had spilled in the window from an elevated station—when I noticed a woman standing who was or should have been on her way to the hospital.

"When are you due?" I asked her. "Thursday," she gasped. "I'm September," I said. "Take my seat." She slumped down and said, with feeling, "You are the first person to give me a seat on the subway since I've been pregnant." Being New

Yorkers, with no sense of personal privacy, we began to exchange subway, taxi, and deli counterman stories. When a man sitting nearby got up to leave, he snarled, "You wanted women's lib, now you got it."

Well, I'm here to say that I did get women's lib, and it is my only fond memory of being pregnant in New York. (Actually, I did find pregnancy useful on opening day at Yankee Stadium, when great swarms of people parted at the sight of me as though I were Charlton Heston in *The Ten Commandments*. But it had a pariah quality that was not totally soothing.)

One evening rush hour during my eighth month I was waiting for a train at Columbus Circle. The loudspeaker was crackling unintelligibly and ominously and there were as many people on the platform as currently live in Santa Barbara, Calif. Suddenly I had the dreadful feeling that I was being surrounded. "To get mugged at a time like this," I thought ruefully. "And this being New York, they'll probably try to take the baby, too." But as I looked around I saw that the people surrounding me were four women, some armed with shoulder bags. "You need protection," one said, and being New Yorkers, they ignored the fact that they did not know one another and joined forces to form a kind of phalanx around me, not unlike those that offensive linemen build around a quarterback.

When the train arrived and the doors opened, they moved forward, with purpose, and I was swept inside, not the least bit bruised. "Looks like a boy," said one with a grin, and as the train began to move, we all grabbed the silver overhead handles and turned away from one another.

NESTING

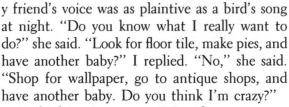y friend's voice was as plaintive as a bird's song at night. "Do you know what I really want to do?" she said. "Look for floor tile, make pies, and have another baby?" I replied. "No," she said. "Shop for wallpaper, go to antique shops, and have another baby. Do you think I'm crazy?"

"I think you're average," I said.

I've had this conversation a half dozen times this winter. The women in question all have one great child and one great job. They're enamored of the kid and tired of the work, in part because it takes too much time away from the kid. That doesn't mean they want to quit, necessarily: "How does four mornings a week sound to you?" another of them said to me one day, rhetorically. But they've all heard the stories about how it's the second baby that's the hole in the bottom of your career boat, plunging you to the depths of domesticity. And they want the second baby. And maybe the boat, too.

But what a lot of them also miss I'll call, for lack of a better term, nesting. It's the wallpaper, the pies, the altogether trivial assemblage of those small component parts that make up life for many of us. Nesting has been traditionally undervalued. This is because nesting has largely been the purview of women.

I, on the other hand, have traditionally overvalued nesting, because I am a crazed nester. It gives me the illusion that the world is a secure and predictable place, with certain pictures on certain walls and certain little piles of pillows on certain beds. I do not always like making soup, fudge, afghans, quilts, and brownies, but I like to at least consider making them. One Saturday at the end of my first pregnancy, I bought fresh flowers for the kitchen, the bedroom, and two of the bathrooms, hung curtains in the baby's room, went to the butcher for lamb chops, and cooked them, along with a cheese soufflé. When the flowers were arranged, the curtains hung, the dinner eaten and the dishes washed, I went into labor. There's a term for this routine in pregnancy books. They call it the nesting instinct, and they warn you about it because if you've been running around buying flowers and lamb chops during the day you'll be too tired to push that night. However, it gave me a certain sense of pride, when the nurse wrote down what I'd last eaten, to be able to say cheese soufflé.

We undervalue nesting now in part because we think of it as a fifties kind of thing, the kind of thing that Mrs. Cleaver did when Wally and the Beav were away at school and she could just sit back with a cup of coffee, go through some pattern books, whip up café curtains for the kitchen and then make some chocolate-chip cookies. Like many of the other things we believe about the mothers in our lives, this one is largely wrong. With five children spread over ten years, my mother had no time for nesting. She didn't have the job, but she didn't have the sitter, either, and it would be years until she got us all in school at the same time. The closest she ever got to paging through wallpaper books and restoring furniture was when she sprung for a diaper pail in a nice pastel.

I've got the sitter, all right, but I also have the job. The last time I looked at wallpaper, I took the kids along, which shows that even fairly intelligent people are sometimes rendered unbelievably stupid by their own competing interests. And I thought seriously about killing three birds with one stone and writing a piece about selecting wallpaper.

Occasionally, over the last ten years, I have met a woman with children in school all day and no job, and I have thought, quite uncharitably and almost reflexively, what in the world does she find to do with herself all day? I don't think that anymore. Now I imagine lunch with a friend, considering slipcovers, doing a little gardening, spending an hour working on dinner before everyone arrives home. That life—of ladies' lunches, of appointments with the upholsterer, and shopping trips stretched to fill the empty hours—is something I ran from with furious little feet when I was growing up. It's something that barely exists now, except among the very rich; it's something that's barely tolerated by men—or by women. It's not that I would like it as a way of life. I'd just like a little fling with it every once in a while.

I'm making this sound a bit too much like an alternative to work. And it's quite distinct from that, and from home decoration, and from having children. (I am sure, for example, that the reason you have such a manic urge to nest the day before you give birth is that it is nature's way of telling you you will not be able to so much as purchase pillowcases for six months.) The word "nesting" is right for it—the sporadic assemblage of small bits and pieces, woven together, arranged correctly, until you are comfortable sitting amidst them. Or perhaps the precise word is something that's almost become an expletive in recent years. I know a fair number of women who wouldn't mind spending just a little more time being homemakers. Making a home. Getting all the fine points right. Surrounding themselves and their families with a cosy twig house of gimcracks and linens and plastic containers filled with good things to eat, in the mistaken belief that this will make everyone happy and safe. It's not a big thing. But I'm tired of big things. Sometimes I just want the time for the little ones, the hours to feather my nest.

THE COMPANY OF WOMEN

t was not until my last year in college that students could live in a coeducational dorm. As with the inauguration of any social experiment, there was a fair amount of press coverage and a lot of alarmist talk, mostly about how we would all wind up swinging from the doorjambs naked and giving birth to unwanted triplets.

This could not have been further from the truth. Instead of orgies, the arrangement bred familiarity. Our tiny tubs of yogurt commingled on the windowsills during the winter. And on a few occasions, a member of one or the other sex ignored the elaborate system of signs rigged up for the bathroom doors and some slight shrieking ensued. It was, in some ways, good preparation for marriage, but not in the way our parents feared.

Nevertheless I came away, unfashionable as it was, thinking that there are still times when I prefer the company of women, particularly when

I am in pajamas. I have recently returned from a week of female bonding, and remain convinced of this. A friend and I flew south with our children. During the week we spent together I took off my shoes, let down my hair, took apart my psyche, cleaned the pieces, and put them together again in much improved condition. I feel like a car that's just had a tuneup. Only another woman could have acted as the mechanic.

And yet it is still widely assumed that a woman who goes off on a trip with other women missed the booking deadline on something else, or is contemplating divorce and has gone away to think things over. Women without men are still thought to be treading water. Men without women have broken loose.

There was much general sympathy for my situation, in which my husband and my friend's husband were too embroiled in their work to lie on the beach and chase children around the swimming pool. We tried to cajole them, but to no avail. "I can't believe the two of you are going alone," said a friend, as though we were fourth graders taking the crosstown bus for the first time.

So we went alone, and each night re-created our personal universes. I cooked, she cleaned. I blathered, she analyzed. Neither felt the need to be sociable, or polite: more than once, we picked up our respective books and started to read at opposite ends of the couch. Most of the time we talked and talked, not in a linear way, but as though we were digging for buried treasure. Why did you feel that way? And what did you say then? What are you going to do about that? How long did that go on? It was an extended version of the ladies' lunches in which we bring our psyches out from inside our purses, lay them on the table, and fold them up again after coffee—except that I shuffled around in a T-shirt and underwear, my ensemble of choice.

It wouldn't have been the same if our husbands had been

along, and not just because I would have had to put on some decent clothes. The conversation would have been more direct, less introspective, less probing for probing's sake. That's not to say I don't have probing conversations with my husband. But they usually revolve around a specific problem; they are what management consultants call goal-directed, not free-floating attempts to make order out of daily life.

I sometimes think the prototype was a conversation we had about the Miranda decision. What was Miranda's first name? I asked. I can't recall, he answered. Was he married? I don't know. Did he have kids? Why is that important? Where did he live? Who cares? Is he still alive? WHO CARES! By the time we had finished the conversation we were about as irritated with each other as two people could be. He was oxford cloth, I embroidery. We simply weren't in the same shirt.

My friends who are women are mostly embroidery, too. Perhaps it is a legacy of childhoods in which it was our mothers who explained why flowers die in the fall, why you can sometimes see the moon during the day, and why boys don't ask you to dance. Perhaps it is a legacy of girlhoods in which it was our mothers, with hours to spend with us, who followed their own mothers' leads and talked about this and that and became, if not the storytellers of our lives, at least the narrators and analysts.

We were not alone in our female bonding at the beach. The older women did the same, sending their husbands off to the golf course, dishing their daughters-in-law. There have been times when I might have felt sympathy and a slight contempt for these women without men, but those were times when I was young and stupid. Those were times when nearly all my friends were men, after the coeducational dorms and before I was at ease with the femaleness in me.

Those times ended when I got a job at an institution as unequivocally male as a pair of black wingtip shoes. When I arrived I was desperate, not to make friends, but to make female friends. One day I met a young woman at the photocopying machine, and struck up a conversation. We became friends; in fact, she is the friend with whom I took the trip. I still remember the lunch at which we narrated the bare bones of our life stories. We have spent the last ten years filling in the blanks, shading, excavating. She probably knows more about some parts of my life than my husband does: nothing critical, just little bits here and there, some of the tiny dots that, taken together, make up the pointillistic picture of our lives.

PUTTING
UP A
GOOD
FRONT

am going to a business lunch, and I look good. I have on a plaid blazer and a print dress; I have successfully mixed patterns, and my jewelry is adequate and real. I am also wearing nice brown boots. They are not exactly right with the clothes, nowhere near as nice as my brown shoes would be, but I am wearing the boots because I am wearing my husband's socks because there are no pantyhose.

Do you understand? If you do, then you are like me. You are Putting Up a Good Front. This is capitalized because it is not a phrase, it is a way of life. I am sorely disappointed to be Putting Up a Good Front at this time of my life. In various other incarnations I believed that the fact that my bed was never made (although I had anemones on the coffee table) and my hems were hemmed with rubber cement (although the skirt was made of imported wool) was a function of either money or age. On the one hand, I believed that if I made a good deal more money I would be able to purchase new things or pay people to tend the old ones. On the other hand, I thought that I was simply a flibbertigibbet, and that sooner or later I would acquire an attention span, and a sewing kit.

Well, I am older and more affluent, and the result has been that I am Putting Up a Good Front better than ever before. I wear nicer clothes, but my scatter pins are still scattered to cover missing buttons. The pantyhose I thought were in my drawer but turned out to be stuffed inside the head of a sock doll were made by a famous designer and were of that wonderful sheer variety that run when you so much as walk past the bureau in which they're nestled. The man's socks were cashmere. I believe they also matched one another, although not my outfit.

It's easy to tell if you are Putting Up a Good Front. For example, your Mastercard will be rejected for cause in elegant restaurants, but you will successfully convince the maître d' to accept a check. Your children will take elaborate sandwiches of English muffins, tomatoes, sliced chicken, and chutney to school because you were too busy preparing Tarte Tatin to buy bread, mayonnaise, and peanut butter. And there are other telltale signs:

—Your living room furniture is upholstered in the currently popular adobe/guacamole/Coppertone shades. Beneath the cushions, there are two felt-tip pens without tops, seventeen raisins, about fifty cents worth of loose change, and the check that you were supposed to mail to the insurance company four months ago. The side of the cushion that is facing down has a long stain of grape juice on it. The arm of the couch has a matching stain, which is covered by a casual hand-loomed throw or an American country quilt.

—Your purse is made of good leather and has a long strap

to be slung stylishly around your shoulders. Inside there is an expensive datebook in which nothing is arranged in alphabetical order, as well as two Lego blocks, the carbons from 142 credit card transactions, a folded crayon drawing purported to be of a witch eating at McDonald's with a dinosaur, and half a bagel with cream cheese. There should never be keys inside your purse, since they might tear the silk lining and enable you to enter your house or your car.

—Your car is a nice car, rather new, with four-wheel drive. However, the maps in the glove compartment are all folded the wrong way, the registration is in the pocket of your coat in your upstairs closet, and there is rarely sufficient gas. If you live in New York, the maps will generally be of New Mexico, Alabama, and downtown Houston. If you live in Seattle, the maps will be of Maine and the Florida Panhandle. In your datebook, however, will be the map you are never without, that all-important map of the London Underground.

All of these things may seem like superficialities, but of course we all know that the purse is the mirror of the soul, and that people whose closets are filled with old tennis racket cases although they have never played tennis are hiding something in their psyches, too. People who are Putting Up a Good Front are often serene, good-humored, and pleasant. So, too, are their refrigerators, until you open the Tupperware.

If you are ever tempted to say to a friend, "God, you really have it all together," this probably means you are dealing with a Good Front, or perhaps even a Great Front. There is a small possibility that a person who appears to have it all together may in fact have it all together, but you won't want to be friends with that person long, anyway. If in doubt, try this test: When you are in their simple but stylish country-warped-beat-up-distressed pine and teeny-tiny cotton prints living room, lovingly smooth the door of the armoire and say, "My, this is pretty." The sentence will be drowned out as the door swings open and things—copies of *Cosmo,* wire whisks, cashmere socks, boots, pantyhose, even a small child—come tumbling out. Just don't do it in my house or you could be injured in the crash.

BLIND AMBITION

hree times last year my elder son told his friends that his mother does not work. This may come as a surprise to you. It certainly surprised me. Yet the neighbors probably share his opinion and, deep in their hearts, so do some of my friends. I know what they mean: I do not hoist the brief-case each morning, take one last pull on the cof-fee cup, and head for an office in a building that looks like a chrome-and-glass étagère.

Instead, I shamble about here in a bathrobe, turn in the robe for sweat pants and, between trips to school and sessions playing trucks on the floor, drop into my office. It contains a file cabi-net, a computer, and a copy of the inspirational "An Octopus and My Mommy Sleeping," ex-ecuted in green and black crayon. When I am blocked, I lean back in my chair and try to figure out which is the octopus and which is me.

It was almost two years ago, while awaiting the imminent birth of my second child, that I de-

cided to start working part time. This would have been un-
thinkable to me when I was younger. At twenty-five I should
have worn a big red A on my chest; it would have stood for
ambition, an ambition so brazen and burning that it would
have reduced Hester Prynne's transgression to pale pink.

When I was in college I baby-sat, using spending money as
my cover. What I would actually do was to look in the college's
client file box for the names of reporters who needed a baby
sitter. I was a good baby sitter. But I also suspected I would
be a good reporter, and I wasn't a bit shy about apprising the
appropriate people of that fact. In this way I got my first job
on a New York newspaper.

I say these things as though they happened to someone else,
because sometimes I feel as though they had.

I am not sure when or why it all changed. It is tempting to
say it is because having children has reordered my priorities.
That is partly true. I still think the quote of the decade was
contained in a letter from a friend of Senator Paul E. Tsongas.
When the senator decided to quit politics, the friend wrote:
"No one on his deathbed ever said, 'I wish I had spent more
time on my business.'"

But the children are not the only factor. My work is a big
part of my life, but experience has taught me that other
things—friends, family, time alone—fill some of my deepest
needs. My youthful infatuation with myself has, happily,
cooled. The inchoate "I want . . . I want" that once filled my
insides, lacking any sort of clear object for that awesome verb,
is muted. I want to do good work. I want to play with my
children. I want to enjoy myself. I want to be happy. I once
wanted to be a personage. Now I am comfortable being a
person.

I am a particularly lucky person. I had gone some distance
up the job ladder before my kids were born. Economically, our
family has been able to absorb my decision. Professionally, I

have benefited richly from it. Many other women's careers have been derailed by part-time work. But a writer's profession is portable. I made the decision to work part time thinking I would stay home and hammer away, solitary and anonymous, on a novel. Now I hammer away on the novel, but I have another job, one without anonymity, one in which I have the company of readers, one I would have killed for when I was twenty-five.

There is a flip side to this, too. I suppose everyone who has ever worked part time has thought: If I can do this much at home in four hours, just think what I could do in an office in ten. I also miss the easy camaraderie of working around other people, in a place devoted primarily to work. There is nothing like ten minutes perched on the corner of a colleague's desk to work out the kinks in a difficult paragraph. There is nothing like a leak in the dishwasher or a surprise attack by a boy armed with *Babar the Elephant* to derail a train of thought.

But I feel now that there is lots of time to get back on track, even though there are never enough hours in a particular day. When I was twenty-five, I always felt as if a bus were coming around the corner with my name on its front bumper, and that I'd damn well better have spent the day working on a good opening sentence for my obit. Now it seems as if there are so many years ahead to pick up where I left off, or backtrack if I need to, or change direction entirely. If I get the forty additional years statisticians say are likely coming to me, I could fit in at least one, maybe two new lifetimes. Sad that only one of those lifetimes can include being the mother of young children.

That is one reason why part-time work is still largely the purview of women. Part of this may be because society still finds it acceptable for us and unacceptable for our male counterparts. There is also a school of thought that says it is because we are finally proving that biology is destiny, that we can't or won't cut the mustard, that men are born with a will to push forward and that women have tried to graft it onto an unwilling tree. I can never remember whether that is the fear-of-success school or the fear-of-failure school. In any case, it doesn't apply to me or to many other women I know. I'm sure not afraid of success and I've learned not to be afraid of failure. The only thing I'm afraid of now is of being someone I don't like much.

In the last month or so my son has finally decided I do work. He says I work upstairs at a "puter." He says Daddy works at an office. When pressed, he occasionally says that Mom writes things and Dad helps people who are in trouble with the law. But mostly he sees it in terms of location: I'm upstairs, Dad's at the office. Perhaps that's how I should think of it, too. This is where I am right now. So far, it feels O.K.

STRETCH MARKS

For most of my life I have pursued a policy toward my body that could best be characterized as benign neglect. From the time I could remember until the time I was fifteen it looked one way, and from the time I was fifteen until I was thirty it looked another way. Then, in the space of two years, I had two children and more weight changes than Ted Kennedy, and my body headed south without me.

This is how I began to work out. I work out for a very simple reason, and it is not because it makes me feel invigorated and refreshed. The people who say that exercise is important because it makes you feel wonderful are the same people who say a mink coat is nice because it keeps you warm. Show me a woman who wears a mink coat to keep warm and who exercises because it feels good and I'll show you Jane Fonda. I wear a mink coat because it is a mink coat, and I work out so that my husband will not gasp when he runs into me in the bathroom and take off with an eighteen-year-old who looks as good out of her clothes as in them. It's as simple as that.

So I go to this gym three times a week, and here is how it works. First I go into the locker room. On the wall is an extremely large photograph of a person named Terri Jones wearing what I can only assume is meant to be a bathing suit. The caption above her body says Slim Strong and Sexy. It is accurate. I check to make sure no one else is in the locker room, then I take my clothes off. As soon as I've done this, one of two people will enter the locker room: either an eighteen-year-old who looks as good out of her clothes as in them who spontaneously confides in me that she is having an affair with a young lawyer whose wife has really gone to seed since she had her two kids, or a fifty-year-old woman who has had nine children, weighs 105 and has abdominal muscles you could bounce a quarter off and who says she can't understand why, maybe it's her metabolism, but she can eat anything she wants, including a pint of Frusen Gladje Swiss chocolate almond candy ice cream, and never gain a pound. So then I go out and exercise.

I do Nautilus. It is a series of fierce-looking machines, each designed, according to this book I have, to exercise some distinct muscle group, which all happen in my case never to have been exercised before. Nautilus was allegedly invented by Arthur Jones, husband of the aforementioned slim strong and sexy Terri, who is his seventeenth wife, or something like that. But I think anyone who comes upon a Nautilus machine suddenly will agree with me that its prototype was clearly invented at some time in history when torture was considered a reasonable alternative to diplomacy. Over each machine is a little drawing of a human body—not mine, of course—with a certain muscle group inked in red. This is so you can recognize immediately the muscle group that is on fire during the time you are using the machine.

There is actually supposed to be a good reason to do Nautilus, and it is supposed to be that it results in toning without bulk: that is, you will look like a dancer, not a defensive lineman. That may be compelling for Terri Jones, but I chose it because it takes me only a little more than a half hour—or what I like to think of as the time an average person burning calories at an average rate would need to read *Where the Wild Things Are, Good Night, Moon* and *The Cat in the Hat* twice—to finish all the machines. It is also not social, like aerobics classes, and will not hold you up to widespread ridicule, like running. I feel about exercise the same way that I feel about a few other things: that there is nothing wrong with it if it is done in private by consenting adults.

Actually, there are some of the Nautilus machines I even like. Call it old-fashioned machisma, but I get a kick out of building biceps. This is a throwback to all those times when my brothers would flex their arms and a mound of muscle would appear, and I would flex mine and nothing would happen, and they'd laugh and go off somewhere to smoke cigarettes and look at dirty pictures. There's a machine to exercise the inner thigh muscles that bears such a remarkable resemblance to a delivery room apparatus that every time I get into it I think someone is going to yell *push!* and I will have another baby. I feel comfortable with that one. On the other hand, there is another machine on which I am supposed to lift a weight straight up in the air and the most I ever manage is to squinch my face up until I look like an infant with bad gas. My instructor explained to me that this is because women have no upper body strength, which probably explains why I've always found it somewhat difficult to carry a toddler and an infant up four flights of stairs with a diaper bag over one shoulder while holding a Big Wheel.

Anyhow, the great thing about working out is that I have met a lot of very nice men. This would be a lot more important if I weren't married and the mother of two. But of course if I was single and looking to meet someone, I would never meet anyone except married men and psychopaths. (This is Murphy's Other Law, named after a Doreen Murphy, who in 1981 had a record eleven bad relationships in one year.) The men I have met seem to really get a kick out of the fact that I work out, not unlike the kick that most of us get out of hearing very small children try to say words like hippopotamus or chauvinist. As one of the men at my gym said, "Most of the people here are guys or women who are uh well hmm umm . . ."

"In good shape," I said.

"I wouldn't have put it like that," he answered.

Because I go to the gym at the same time on the same days, I actually see the same men over and over again. One or two of them are high school students, which I find truly remarkable. When I was in high school, it was a big deal if a guy had shoulders, never mind muscles. So when I'm finished I go back into the locker room and take a shower. The eighteen-year-old is usually in there, and sometimes she'll say something like, "Oh, that's what stretch marks look like." Then I put on my clothes and go home by the route that does not pass Dunkin' Donuts. The bottom line is that I really hate to exercise, but I have found on balance that this working out is all worth it. One day we were walking down the street and one of the guys from my gym—it was actually one of the high school guys, the one with the great pecs—walked by and said, "How ya doing?" My husband said, "Who the hell is that guy?" and I knew that Nautilus had already made a big difference in my life.

LOVING
A
MAN

HUSBANDS AND BOYFRIENDS

watched *Gone With the Wind* on television recently. It's my favorite movie. It's hokey, it's predictable, the color's lurid, I throw balled-up tissues at Olivia de Haviland when she's on screen. I love it. Each time I see it I notice something new.

This time, I noticed that in some ways it perfectly illustrates one of the great truths about men. Most men fall into one of two categories for the purpose of relationships: Husband or Boyfriend. These are not literal classifications based on marital status, just the best I can do. (I once classified them as the Good Guy and the Louse, which was an oversimplification made when I was depressed, menwise, and before I had admitted that I found the Lice much more interesting than their nobler brothers.)

Ashley Wilkes is a classic Husband: upright, dependable, prone neither to wild partying nor to gross flirtation. He will show up for dinner on time and be the kind of father a kid can depend on for lots of meaty talks about life and honor.

Rhett Butler is, of course, vintage Boyfriend: entertaining, unprincipled, with a roving eye and a wickedly expressive brow above it. I've watched Scarlett turn around and see him for the first time at the bottom of the staircase at Twelve Oaks plantation at least a hundred times. "He looks as if—as if he knows what I look like without my shimmy," she says, one of the few insightful things she says in the first half of the film, before she eats the radish and swears that she'll never be hungry again. And still my heart stops and I have trouble breathing. Give a damn? You bet I do.

This is because, unlike the obtuse Scarlett, I have never had any difficulty deciding between the Boyfriend and the Husband. Perhaps it is the way I was raised. My mother told me I should marry someone who could dance and who would make me laugh. She also said I should find somebody who wouldn't bore me. She never said a word about a good provider. It was good advice, as far as it went, but since my mother had married a Boyfriend, it only went so far.

Of course, I married a Boyfriend, too, fell for him like a ton of bricks the first time I saw him wearing a sport coat with blue jeans and a wicked grin. I can't say I've never regretted it, because there have been times when I've wanted to turn him in for Ward Cleaver. But the truth is that if I had it to do over again, I would do it exactly the same way.

It's sometimes hard to accept this, although God knows why. Boyfriends rarely pretend to be Husbands. But lots of women fall for someone who is the life of the party, a dancing fool who has a weak spot for women, and then become enraged when they find themselves married to someone who is the life of the party, a dancing fool who has a weak spot for women. They expect matrimony to turn Jack Nicholson into Alan Alda. Yet they know that if they woke up in bed one morning with

Alan Alda, they'd soon yearn with all their hearts for just a little *Sturm und Drang,* a little rock 'n' roll.

I don't mean to sound so down on Husbands. I think these are good times for them, with women marrying later in life and actively seeking stability and maturity in a man. Teenage girls have no interest in anything but Boyfriends, and women who marry early are often overly enamored of the kind of man who looks great in wedding pictures and passes the maid of honor his telephone number. But women who have been around a bit are, I think, more likely to see the virtues in a Husband.

A Husband provides a shoulder to lean on; when you lean on a Boyfriend's shoulder he may very well say, "You're wrinkling my jacket." You know what you are getting with a Husband, and at a time in your life when you've had too many unpleasant surprises—a man who demanded a commitment and then moved to L.A. the minute he got one, another who insisted he wanted to get married and then married his ex-girlfriend the day after you split—knowledge is power. You think you know what you are getting with a Boyfriend, but they're a little like kaleidoscopes: infinite permutations, many of them garish.

Men can work their own alchemy on the mix, too. The most obvious manifestation of the much ballyhooed midlife crisis is that the longtime Husband turns into a Boyfriend, starts driving a red car, wearing leather pants, and talking knowledgeably about the kinds of bands that generally hit the Top 10 with songs with only three words in them ("Yeah," "Love," and "Baby"). There are also a few documented cases of Boyfriends turning into Husbands, although not many. These can usually be linked to career changes, promotions, and fatherhood. (Even Rhett started to act pretty straight after Bonnie was born.)

My husband, a bred-in-the-bone Boyfriend, was terrified of this aspect of having children, convinced that on the morning after our first son was born he would awaken with a drawerful of pajamas and cardigan sweaters and the urge to say things like, "Now, son, I think we should have a little talk about that." Not a chance. His most recent foray into fatherhood was to teach both his children the words to "You Give Love a Bad Name." The eldest can also play air guitar along with the song. On the one hand, I hate "You Give Love a Bad Name," although my children sing it rather well. On the other hand, my husband would not think twice about scandalizing a Confederate ball by bidding $150 in gold to dance with me. And, like Scarlett, when someone said, "She will not consider it, sir," I know what I would say without a moment's hesitation: "Oh, yes, I will."

AIR-CONDITIONING

very family has its divisions. There are the people who like white meat and the people who like dark meat, the people who like the country and the people who like the city, the people who like showers and the people who like baths, the people who like electric blankets and the people who know deep down that some night some quirk of wiring is going to stun them like a bug flying into one of those purple bug lights.

Each summer my thoughts turn to still another division between family members, the one between people who like air-conditioning and people who don't. Such a division exists right here within my own family, in this very house, which is, as I write this, about 7 billion degrees Fahrenheit. Hotter than the sun's surface. Hotter than the planet Mars. Hotter than Michael Jackson was a scant few years ago.

I am the person in this family who thinks that air-conditioning is one of the more wonderful modern inventions, right up there with hot rollers and Cuisinarts. I think air-conditioning feels good in the summer, just as heat (not, I repeat not, electric-blanket heat) feels good in the winter.

The other adult in this family is opposed to air-conditioning. The other adult is six feet tall and wears a tie. Most important, he is a lawyer, so he can make almost anything sound at once logical and abstruse. So far, he has won. The children nap in their tiny saunas, the A-B-C wallpaper peeling and blistering. There is perspiration on my computer screen.

This has put a strain on the family. In the car, which has air-conditioning only because it was bought off the lot, options included, the children are startled from their first comfortable sleep of the season by my voice, screaming, as we pass a hardware store:

"BUY AN AIR-CONDITIONER!"

No reply. We speed down the highway.

The other adult will insist that he has already bought an air-conditioner. It cools one floor of a four-story row house. He says he is not opposed to air-conditioning qua air-conditioning, just air-conditioning in rooms where people sleep: if I start to doze off in the living room it becomes out-of-bounds.

In an apartment across the street one of our neighbors got laryngitis sleeping in an air-conditioned room. "If you have the slightest iota of humanity," I told her, "you will not say anything to him." She nodded. She couldn't speak anyhow. Inevitably, the other adult in our family ran into her and tried to engage her in conversation. When he came inside the house (as hot as a mirror lying on the ground at the equator) he was smiling. "Told you," he said warmly. I appealed to my mother-in-law. The other adult said that if no air-conditioning had been good enough for her sons when they were little, no air-conditioning was good enough for ours.

"This is a lie," my mother-in-law said coolly, sitting in the living room of a condominium that has central air-conditioning. "In the beginning we had one air-conditioner downstairs. On hot nights the boys would come down and sleep on the floor. Later we got air-conditioners for the entire house."

"Later they bought a fake Christmas tree, too," my husband said hotly, when confronted with this.

You may be saying to yourself, Hey, why doesn't she go out and buy an air-conditioner herself? She just sent $197 to Benetton for fall fashions that are too young-looking for her. She has money. Don't tell me she's waiting for (chortle, snicker, frown) MALE APPROVAL?

Well, she doesn't go out and buy one because she can't get the thing into the house, O.K.? It weighs a ton. I practiced on the one we already have. I can't lift even one end of it. And I am up to forty pounds on the Nautilus biceps-triceps sequence. Otherwise I would buy one, stick it in the window, and sweat out the other adult's remarks for the next twenty, twenty-five-years.

I thought of appealing to other men for help, but here are my options: my brothers (read my husband's brothers-in-law), my brothers-in-law (my husband's brothers), his friends (right), my friends (who are also his friends). I know what would happen. They come in, they stand around hitting one another's upper arms and shuffling their feet and making male bonding moves and perspiring profusely, and finally some brave soul says: "Yo. We don't think he'd like it, you know?" Then they drink my beer and leave.

So here I am surrounded by fans, their big dull blades pushing warm air from one end of the house to another. It occurs to me that I missed my big chance. Twice I've been pregnant in this kind of weather, a water balloon with feet, and I did not take the opportunity to complain enough. Now I have no leverage. The children are good-tempered and they like to watch the fans go round and round. The older one thinks sweat is fun because it tastes like salt.

I think back to the days when I was renovating this old house and the plumber was putting in the new furnace. "Baseboard heat?" I remember him saying. "You could put in central air." I looked around at my moldings and said "Nah." Now every time I see his truck go by I want to leap out of the window of this house (as hot as those chilies lying in wait in Szechuan food) and yell "COME BACK."

The other adult in the family drinks a beer and watches the ball game. "There are only three or four days of the year when you really need air-conditioning," he says evenly. I fan myself with a copy of *Vogue* and wonder if climate control is grounds for divorce in this state. He also likes electric blankets.

"I DON'T LIKE THAT NIGHTGOWN"

have been married for almost ten years to the same person. Sometimes it's hard for me to believe. Neither of us were sure that any human being could be expected to live over the long haul with anyone as stubborn, opinionated, and difficult as the other. Somehow it has worked, and it is not a gross exageration to say that this is partly due to the fact that I am a much better cook than he is, and he tells much better jokes than I do.

A lot of people don't understand how important these little things are to a marriage. I realized this when I was reading a magazine article about bachelors, many of whom were participating in organized sports instead of having relationships with women, just like their football coaches told them they should do when they were seventeen. Many of these bachelors seemed to think that it would take a lot of compromise and change on the part of both partners to stay married. Nothing could be farther from the truth. One touchstone of marriage is security, and nothing makes you feel more secure than knowing exactly what another person is going to say or do at any given time. If my husband just cut into a slightly pink pork chop and scoffed it down, instead of holding a piece up at eye level, looking at it as though it was a murder suspect, and saying, "Is this cooked enough?"—well, I'd become pretty suspicious, I can tell you that.

I felt this sense of continuity just the other night. It was a cold night, a wintry night, and I was getting ready to go to sleep when my husband said, "I don't like that nightgown." And once again I felt that magic little thrill you always get when you realize that some things in your life are immutable. It was a flannel nightgown I was wearing, one of those little numbers that looks like a fallout shelter and is designed to reveal only that the body beneath possesses ankles. It's warm and comfortable, but I've always known, deep in my heart, that the only person who would consider it seductive would be Buddy Ebsen. Once a year my husband looks at one of these things and says, "I don't like that nightgown." I guess if I was what my grandmother used to call a dutiful wife, I wouldn't wear them. But just think how out-of-kilter that would throw my husband's whole existence.

Luckily neither of us ever has to go for long without these little touchstones that keep our relationship solid. More than that, I think they bring home to me constantly the differences between men and women. These are important to keep in mind, because the clearest explanation for the failure of any marriage is that the two people are incompatible—that is, that one is male and the other female. There are all those times when I've purchased a new dress for a special occasion and my husband has glimpsed those telltale price tags in the trash. "Did you need a new dress?" he will always say, once again illustrating the gender-based distinction between necessity and desire. Or there's the ever-popular "You look fine without makeup," usually uttered when I am applying eyeliner five minutes after he has determined we should be in the car. To which the obvious answer is, "The only place I've ever gone without makeup is to the recovery room." I think it's worth noting that I was once at a party at which a man said quite loudly, "You look fine without makeup" and eight women turned around, each thinking it was their husband.

(Of course, these things can backfire on you, too. If I ever am divorced by my husband, for example, it will probably be because I have made it a practice throughout my life never to put the caps back on things. With those grounds and the right judge, he could probably get the kids, the house, the dogs, and all the toothpaste tubes, as well as the jar of mayonnaise that has tinfoil molded over the opening.)

However, I am beginning to think that the flannel nightgown is larger than this, figuratively as well as literally. Perhaps it is an extended metaphor for the difference between what men want from a marriage, and what women want. There's a real temptation to say that women want a relationship that is secure, comfortable, and enduring, while men are really looking for excitement, sex, and black lace. Obviously those are stereotypes. Lots of the bachelors in this magazine piece seemed to be interested in a secure relationship, although some of them had settled for touch football instead. I even have one friend, who previously had the kind of lingerie collection usually confined to a Victoria's Secret catalogue, who fell in love with a man who thinks flannel nightgowns are sexy, in the way the librarian with the bun and the glasses turns out to be something else entirely once she takes her hairpins out. (I know your next question. Forget it. This man is not available. He is taken.) And I know lots of women are interested in having some excitement in their lives, although a great many of the single women I know wish that excitement didn't so often include cheating, lying, and uncomfortable undergarments.

It's a little late for me to fall in love with a man who likes cotton flannel and the allure of the dowdy. I'm already taken, too. And I know all his little winning ways, and he knows mine. I believe this is the secret to a successful marriage. It beats me why someone like Madonna, for example, would think she had irreconcilable differences with Sean Penn. Now there's a man you can count on: point a camera and he throws a punch, as predictable and consistent as can be, still spitting and swearing and indulging in fisticuffs, the same guy today as he was the day she married him. I like a certain reliability in a man, and I've got it. I put a plate of radicchio salad on the table, step back, and count to five. "What is this stuff?" my husband says suspiciously, poking it with his fork. It warms my heart.

MARRIED

ach night for the last week, as I have gone out to walk the dogs or leave the trash at the curb, the boy and girl have been shadows in the doorway of the house next door. Even when it was raining, lightning bisecting the sky, they were there, entangled in one of those kisses that last forever, that end only when the oxygen supply gives out. One night the boy spoke as the dogs sniffed at the steps below. "Do you know how much I love this girl?" he asked, a rhetorical boast to a middle-aged stranger.

"Oh, God," I said, tugging on the leashes, and though the lovers might have thought my response indicated disapproval, it was really the shock of recognition, sharp and silver as the lightning. I remember being in love like this. Entering into a state more like a tropical disease than a relationship, listening to one catchy piece of bubble-gum music over and over again and getting the same odd feeling in the stomach and the chest. When I was in high school, the song was by the Beach Boys, "Wouldn't It Be Nice": "Though it's gonna make it that much better/When we can say goodnight and stay together." The big payoff. Not so much sex, at least for the girls, as a kind of mythical domesticity: napkins and matching place mats, unlimited kissing, no adults, flowers every day. What our parents referred to as playing house.

It's getting on to ten years that I've been married. I'm not sure when I realized that reality was going to be both something less and something much more. Luckily many of us know this before we marry, or there would be even more disasters than we now suffer through, many more people packing away an expensive wedding album in some corner of the basement where, it is hoped, it will mildew.

When I was younger, I tended to fall in love with just one thing: a kind of bravado, a certain smile. (The girl in the doorway, I am convinced, has fallen for blond hair and a crooked grin.) I even fell in love with a certain set of bony shoulders in a sport jacket years ago. But unlike a lot of my friends, who went through more than a few Mr. Wrongs and have now settled down with Mr. Maybe, I married the person inside the sport jacket. And I held on like a dog with a bone to a love affair between a girl whose idea of awesome responsibility was a psych midterm and a boy who painted his dorm room black, long after that boy and girl were gone. I held onto what has been going on in that doorway long past the time when I was really too old to believe in magic.

Truth is, I still believe in magic, and it's still there, although there's no point denying that it is occasionally submerged beneath a welter of cereal bowls, dirty shirts, late nights, early mornings, and all the other everyday things that bubble-gum music never reflects. But what I didn't know about marriage, the less magical parts of it, has become perhaps more important to me. Now we have history as well as chemistry. An enormous part of my past does not exist without my husband. An enormous part of my present, too. I still feel somehow that things do not really happen to me unless I have told them to him. I don't mean this nonsense about being best friends, which I have never been able to cotton to; our relationship is too judgmental, too demanding, too prickly to have much in common with the quiet waters of friendship. Like emotional acupuncturists, we know just where to put the needle. And do.

But we are each other's family. And while I know people who have cut their families loose, who think them insignificant or too troublesome to be part of their lives, I am not one of those people. I came late to the discovery that we would be related by marriage. I once made a fool of myself in front of a friend in the emergency room of a small resort hospital after my husband's stomach and a bad fried clam had had an unfortunate meeting. "Are either of you related to him?" the nurse asked, and we both shook our heads until our friend prodded me gently in the side. "Oh, well, I'm his wife," I said.

There is something so settled and stodgy about turning a great romance into next of kin on an emergency room form, and something so soothing and special, too. I suppose that is what I find so dreadful about divorce; lovers are supposed to leave you in the lurch, but your family is supposed to stick by you forever. "You can pick your friends, but you can't pick your relations," the folksy folks always say. Ah, but in this one case you can. You just don't realize it at the time.

What does it mean that I do not envy the two of them, standing in the doorway, locked together like Romeo and Juliet in the tomb? I suppose when I was their age I would have assumed it meant that I was old and desiccated. But of course what has really happened is that I know the difference now between dedication and infatuation.

That doesn't mean I don't still get an enormous kick out of infatuation: the exciting ephemera, the punch in the stomach, the adrenaline to the heart. At a cocktail party the other night I looked across a crowded room and was taken by a stranger, in half profile, a handsome, terribly young-looking man with a halo of backlighted curls. And then he turned and I realized that it was the stranger I am married to, the beneficiary on my insurance policy, the sport jacket, the love of my life.

BECOMING
A
MOTHER

UNDERSTUDY

hen I was nineteen years old, the temporary female caretaker of four younger siblings and a split-level house on a corner plot in the suburbs and desperate to get back to college, I put an advertisement in the local paper. It read:

> **HOUSEKEEPER**
> to cook and clean for five children.
> Own room.
> References required.

At the time I was surprised that only one person called. (Now, I am amazed that anyone did.) I arranged an interview with the sole applicant and read the letters from the past employers that she carried in her purse. Then I hired her. Her name was Ida. She moved in with a collection of wigs, a half-dozen housecoats with snaps up the front, and a Bible with a black Leatherette cover. She was my salvation.

Ida is blind now, and lives in Florida. "Girl," she said at the christening of my second child, her sinewy hand curled around that of the woman who was caring for my children, "if the Lord had not taken my eyes you'd be out of a job." And she was right. Ida was perfect. She was a passable cook, a marvelous raconteur, and a good sport. Most important, she believed she was on a mission from God. One day in her second week of work, a strong wind blew through the open windows of our house and Ida took it to be the meteorological incarnation of my deceased mother. It did no good to mention that my mother was not the strong-wind type; Ida felt that she had been called and that God had charged her with looking after us.

I have been thinking of Ida lately because the person who most recently helped with my children left us in the lurch. I like to think that I would not be so angry if she had handled it better, but that is a delusion. When Kay, who after two years with my children had become my friend as well as theirs, gave me plenty of time to plan for her departure, I was irrationally enraged. How dare she leave, I thought, not soothed by her willingness to stay until I found someone else. And when, after nearly a year, Margaret suddenly decided to move on, I thought the same: How dare she abandon my children, my wonderful, well-behaved, happy little boys? I didn't allow my-self to think of the other side of that question: How dare I?

That isn't fair, exactly; it has become clear to me that my kids do very well with a judicious mixture of Mommy and someone else, and that I do very well with that mixture, too. But still, when it collapses I become aware of how tenuous this structure is, of how my work life is built on sand.

My husband is more businesslike about all this, but then, he is more removed from all this. One of our friends was flabber-gasted, two weeks after Margaret had begun working for us, to find out that he had never met her. Despite all our best efforts

at an equitable distribution of parenting, it seems that the
public perception, and the private one, too, is that I have hired
these people to do my job. I work, and they work at the life
that takes place while I am working. I hold the money, they
hold the power to give me peace of mind while I make the
money. No matter how good the relationship between us, we
are ultimately at each other's mercy, which is not a comfortable
place to be.

I felt helpless and at sea when I realized that Margaret would
not be coming anymore, and I am not a person who feels that
way often. Put an advertisement in the paper, my husband said,
but it was not as simple as he made it out to be, like hiring a
carpenter. There is not even a name for what I am searching
for. Nanny? Too starchy and British. Sitter? Too transient to
describe someone who (please God) shows up every morning.
Housekeeper? If it was the house that needed looking after, I
could be calm right now. Mother? Bite your tongue! What I
want is what I had with Ida, the illusion of mother, the feeling
of total care without the total emotional commitment on the
part of those cared for. I want an understudy, someone who
knows the role but will step aside for me at performances. I
want a paid member of the family. I want permission to sometimes go my own way.

I've heard all the horror stories, but somehow I've been very
lucky in my searches: first Kay, smart and funny and full of an
endless supply of silly nursery songs, the disenchanted former
manager of a rock-and-roll band; then Margaret, the mother of
four grown sons, warm and nurturing even if she did take off
on me. Now it is Sandy, quite literally the girl next door, more
like a big sister than a surrogate mother, who carts the kids off
to Burger King and teaches them how to moonwalk. My sons,
who never called any of them Mommy by mistake, loved them
while they were around and yet let them go with equanimity.
Each of these women was discreet enough not to mention the

first step or the first word if it took place while I was away from home.

Of course, between one leaving and the other arriving, I have thought the same thing: Do it yourself. No one can do it as well as you. That's not true, actually; each one of them did certain things better than I did, gave something that I simply don't have in me. It is hard to find someone who will give your children a feeling of security while it lasts and not wound them too much when it is finished, who will treat those children as if they were her own, but knows—and never forgets—that they are yours.

It is a paradoxical relationship. And, if the truth be told, when I put the advertisement in the paper what I really want to write is PERSON WANTED: Must be on a mission from God.

THE MOTHER OF SONS

n the bottom drawer of the changing table, beneath the snowsuits and the hats, is a pink-and-white striped dress with a white pinafore. It is a size twelve months. The wife of one of my husband's law partners sent it, when my first child's somewhat androgynous name and my stubborn feminist refusal to put a colored ribbon on the birth announcements led her to the conclusion that Quindlen Krovatin was a girl. He was not. I wrote in the thank-you note that I would return the dress for a jogging suit or a pair of overalls, but I never did, and there it lies in the drawer, with the tissue still stuffed inside it, like some limp little body. It has been joined by a pair of white socks with pink birds on the cuffs and a pink cardigan sweater.

There she stays, my phantom daughter, equal parts of cotton, wool, and fantasy. For I am the mother of sons. Somehow I always knew it would be so. Never fastidious, always a pal or a sister, a haphazard fan of both the Yankees' uniforms and their bullpen, I was the girl always taken aside by some boy who confessed his love for someone remote, tremulous, girly—that is, someone else.

I have been mothering boys all my life, from brothers to boyfriends. The only girl I ever mothered was my sister, who has turned out awfully well, but it was a struggle for me. I remember one long drive to the Y, when she was nine and I nineteen, when I delivered a long-rehearsed explanation of copulation and conception, as one of the most torturous moments of my life. She says it never happened. Who knows which of us is right? The fact is that, rightly or wrongly, with a boy it would have been more matter-of-fact for me, less a lesson in life than biology. Try as I might not to do so, perhaps I am perpetuating stereotypes. I am the mother of boys the way we've long thought of boys as being. In fact, it seems to me now, the way they are.

Once it was fashionable to suggest that there were no differences between little boys and little girls; in fact, I was one of the people doing the suggesting. But I don't believe that anymore. I'm not sure whether we treat them differently from the moment those little pink or blue signs are plastered on the maternity ward bassinets, or whether it is hormones, or whether it is some mysterious alchemy like puppy dogs' tails and sugar and spice, but when we watch our children from the park bench at the playground, I and the other mothers can't help noticing that something is different. It is not so much that at school the girls head toward the tables and chairs and modeling clay and crayons, while the boys career down the slides and build with blocks, although all of us remark on it. It is that the girls seem reactive, subjective, measuring reactions, gauging responses. My son, a simple machine, direct, transparent, is as like them as a hammer is like a Swiss watch.

And so I am the other in my family. They are all three like

this, hammers to my Swiss watch. My husband and my two young sons will all wear the same sort of underwear, and they will all have the same last name, and I can see sometimes, although one is still at the age when he is little more than a collection of firing synapses, that they sometimes think there is something a little strange about me. But I do not feel lonely, although strangers on the street feel compelled to feel sorry for me and say that maybe next time I'll have a girl.

That would be nice, but in some ways more difficult. The other day a friend called and told me that her newly adolescent daughter, with whom she had been only moments before the best of friends, had just told her to do something that, included in a movie, would change its rating from PG to R. From what I've seen of the world, her son will not do that. Or as my mother-in-law, the mother of six boys—and never mind the sympathy, because she likes it just fine—said to me, "My boys have respect for me." If my sons are like a good many others I know, they'll reach a point when they will measure themselves against their father and find him wanting: a has-been, a never-was, a sellout, a fat cat. My husband has sufficient backbone to stand up to those few years when his children will preoccupy themselves with what a flimsy figure of a man he is and how they will never be like him. Falling in the toilet occasionally because someone has forgotten to put the seat down will be a small price for me to pay for taking a pass on that.

This is not to say that I will abdicate the tough-guy stance with my boys. (I recall my brother sitting in his room, his face dark, after he had been suspended from school. "Dad is going to kill you," I said. "I don't care about Dad," he said. "I just don't want HER to cry.") And I am already at work on making them warm and caring and easy with the idea of women as intellectual and professional equals. In short, I intend to make some nice woman a wonderful husband. I just think I am more naturally inclined toward doing that, rather than making the nice woman herself.

Of course, this raises the question of why I keep the dress. Why didn't I return it for something that would be suitable for my boys? It would be easy to say that a little bit of hope springs eternal, that deep down I still want to have a daughter and I'm hedging my bets. It would be easy, but it wouldn't be true. I have a funny kind of intuitive feeling—reinforced, perhaps, by the sheer numerical force of my husband's family—that my other children, if they come, will be boys, too.

The dress is really for me. It reminds me of one of those museum exhibits—a party dress circa 1860, the school uniform of an upper-class Victorian girl, those somewhat sad, faded relics of another time, another place. The little collection in the bottom drawer is a kind of monument: to a little girl raised as his oldest son by a man who swore his firstborn would be a boy and never changed his mind; to the girl at the all-girls' school who was lucky enough to be cast as Peter Pan or Hamlet and only for a minute yearned for Wendy's nightdress or Ophelia's robes; to a teenager who was one of the boys and always a little outside the sorority of her own kind. I suppose it reflects all the ambivalence of a tough little girl who had disdain for girly girls and yet somewhere yearned to be one herself. It is for the sort of girl I never was and the kind of woman I may never be, for a place inside me I only lately knew I had when I found it empty and unlikely to be filled.

TAG SALE

There is nothing like a tag sale to force you to confront the hard choices in life. To junk the class notes from Introduction to Psychology and give away the trunk that houses them; to stare with hard, unromantic eyes at the cake plate your husband's great-aunt gave you as a wedding present and tote it out to the car; to look upon a size 8 suit and accept for all time that the body it fits is no longer yours—these things mark milestones, besides providing much-needed closet space.

The nursery school is having a tag sale. The school hall is filled with merchandise: bad afghans, ill-conceived table lamps, remaindered books. Amid it all are the artifacts of those families that consider themselves complete. There is a changing table, an assortment of stretch suits in pastel colors, a crop of crib bumpers. Tag sales are a godsend when the gestating is through; there is nothing more cumbersome or superfluous than a crib around the house when your former babies are out tearing up the playground, their T-shirts mottled with ice cream, dirt, and a bit of blood.

I know this because the top floor of my house is filled with items gathering dust, with down-at-the-heel walkers and baby gates and snowsuits size 9 months. They are not going to the tag sale. I have looked and looked at them, dumped boxes of old overalls onto the floor and then packed them up again. The tag sale makes clear to me, more clear than watching my kids sleep or explaining to them why llamas spit, that I am not ready to say I am finished with having babies. It may be that I will never have more than these two children, for reasons logical or biological. And certainly, they would be sufficient for me. But if I give away the baby things, I am giving away a part of my life that I am not yet ready to relinquish.

It is so seductive, this part, this making someone out of nothing. It feels so important, and so powerful, which is one of the reasons young girls who feel unimportant and powerless so often embrace it, without a thought to all the work and trouble that comes later. There is a lot of work and trouble, and that is why so many of my friends are happy to call a halt to their baby making. Ecstatic to have them, ecstatic to have it over with, they have pushed the playpen with glee into the back of someone else's van, gone to their tubal ligations and vasectomies with great happiness. Time to move on.

I am rotten at moving on. There was a time right after college when I gave lots of odd little parties, with not enough chairs and people sitting on the floor and food like Welsh rarebit or chipped beef. What I really needed was a chafing dish with a little candle underneath to keep all this slop warm, but I could not buy one. I was convinced that if I bought a chafing dish, it would somehow mean I would never get married. A chafing dish is a wedding present. (In fact, I got three as wedding presents. I used one once. I don't prepare chafing-dish meals anymore. I gave one dish to the tag sale last year.

I am keeping the two others in case my kids want to have Welsh rarebit parties after they go skating on cold winter days when they are teenagers. But don't hold your breath.)

Now, I cannot get past the changing pads and the diaper bags. This is not about possessions; I could give away all my baby things and have another baby anyway. It is about what the possessions represent. Last year, someone turned over a portable typewriter to the tag sale, telling herself once and for all that she was never going to be a novelist. It was a shabby typewriter and brought five dollars; only five dollars for what had once been an open door, a possibility, the turn of the kaleidoscope that could alter the pattern of someone's life forever. Then it was put up for sale, and it was nothing but a typewriter in a pale-blue case.

I don't see so many open doors anymore, so many ways to change the pattern, alter my life and the world. I don't want a divorce, and I don't want to move. I have reluctantly accepted the fact that I am not going to follow any alternative career paths, that I am not going to medical school. But I want to leave this particular door to the future open. Some of the women I know are further along; they are convinced that they have stopped at two children, or three, or one, happy and content. And yet . . . and yet. "I sometimes still think about it," one woman said the other day, amid the perpetual chaos of her living room. "And then I think that I still can if I want to." Then she laid the flat of her hand on her abdomen, which will never be taut again.

Knowing that I still can, knowing that I might, knowing that I will: these are all very different things. I will be thirty-five-years old this summer. Someday a time will come when the apparatus that has worked so well will no longer work for me. For all I know, that time came last month, or will come this year, or will not come for a long, long time. But that will be an ending reached without my acquiescence. This one requires my cooperation. And as I look into a box of crib sheets, yellow with milk stains, yellowing just a bit with age, I know that I cannot cooperate right now. I have a feeling of possibility within me that means too much to give away. I could use the closet space, but right now it is something else I need much, much more.

MOTHER'S DAY

or several years after my mother's death, I felt about Mother's Day the way I suppose recently divorced people feel about Valentine's Day. It seemed to be an organized effort by the immediate world to spit in my eye, and I gladly would have set fire to every card in every card rack in every card shop in town. In time, the rage abated, and what remained in its place was an emotionless distance. Mother's Day became much like Passover, a holiday that people like me did not celebrate.

Secretly, I suspected that I would be reconciled to it someday, when I had children, when I was a mother. This conclusion seemed logical and sensible and was completely wrong. Mother's Day is still fraught with strong emotion, if only because each year I feel like a fraud. It is undeniable that I have given birth to two children; I remember both occasions quite vividly. But the orchid corsage, the baby-pink card with the big

M in curly script, the burnt toast on a tray in bed—they belong
to someone else, some other kind of person, some sort of moral
authority. They belong to Mother, and each of us knows quite
well who that person is, and always will be.

That person is a concept. I suppose that is where it all goes
wrong. I know few people who have managed to separate the
two. My friends speak about their mothers, about their
manipulations and criticisms and pointed remarks, and when
I meet these same women I can recognize very little of them
in the child's description. They usually seem intelligent,
thoughtful, kind. But I am not in a position to judge. To me
they are simply people, not some lifelong foil, a yardstick by
which to measure myself, to publicly find Mother wanting, to
privately find the fault within.

And yet I know the feeling. Although she was long dead
when I had my children, my mother and I were then somehow
equals, peers, alike in my mind. That was the most disconcert-
ing feeling of my life. I was part of a generation of women so
different from their mothers as to sometimes be a palpable
insult, daughters who were perhaps as likely to model themselves on the male parent as the female one. For all of my life
my mother had been the other: I was aggressive, she was
passive. (Perhaps simply reserved?) I was intellectual, she was
not. (Perhaps not given the opportunity?) I was gregarious, she
was shy. (Perhaps simply more selective in her attachments?)
At a family gathering recently, several people I have not seen
since I was a girl approached and said they knew who I was
because I looked exactly like my mother. I was chilled to the
bone. How dare they? How dare they consign me to her shoes?
How dare they allow me to fill them?

But in some sense I have slipped into them simply by having
children of my own. Nearly every day an echo of my mother's
mothering wafts by me, like the aroma of soup simmering on
a stove down the street. Even as we swear we will not do some

of the horrible things they did, not pull the thumb like a cork from our children's mouths, not demand that they clean their plates, our mothers' words come full-blown out of our mouths, usually in anger: "If you do that it will be the last thing you do." "You've got another think coming." "Over my dead body." "Because I said so, that's why." Even as we enumerate their shortcomings, the rigor of raising children ourselves makes clear to us our mothers' incredible strength. We fear both. If they are not strong, who will protect us? If they are not imperfect, how can we equal them?

Perhaps those conflicting emotions help us reconcile ourselves to our mothers, make us able to apprehend the shadow of a human being who is just raising other human beings the best she can, beneath the terrible weight of the concept. In the beginning it is difficult. I have envied my friends who have had their mothers to help them with new babies, then felt the envy evaporate at the distress and doubt my friends sometimes felt about who was really the mother here. "No girl becomes a woman until she has lost her mother," someone once told me. And there was the proof: women reduced to children again in a way I never could be.

Yet it is having children that can smooth the relationship, too. Mother and daughter are now equals. That is hard to imagine, even harder to accept, for among other things, it means realizing that your own mother felt this way, too—unsure of herself, weak in the knees, terrified about what in the world to do with you. It means accepting that she was tired, inept, sometimes stupid; that she, too, sat in the dark at 2:00 A.M. with a child shrieking across the hall and no clue to the child's trouble.

Most of this has little to do with the specific women involved. In my case that is certainly true. This firestorm is not about one sweet, gentle mother, perhaps tough and demanding inside, and one tough, demanding daughter, now sweet and gentle with her own children. It has to do with Mother with a capital M: someone we are afraid to be and afraid that we can never be. It has to do with a torch being passed, with finding it too hot to hold, with looking up at the person who has given it to you and accepting that, without it, she is no Valkyrie, just a woman muddling through, much like me, much like you.

RAISING

A

CHILD

THE
BIRTHDAY-
PARTY
WARS

have returned from the birthday-party wars. My side lost. Balloons were broken, jelly sandwiches fell jelly-side down on wall-to-wall carpets, the wine for the adults ran out. Two of the same dinosaurs were received as gifts. (They were stegosauruses.) There were whistles as party favors in violation of decent human standards. All around us the battle raged. This is why the birth process is roughly commensurate to participating in a triathalon in hell: to prepare parents for the birthday parties. In the thick of one celebration I took a cleansing breath and then panted. It did not help. I realized the following:

—Piñatas are the only things in life that are truly unbreakable. You can knock them, you can hit them, you can beat them with a stick, yet they continue to swing through the air: ruffled crepe paper, papier-mâché, and a smile. Dumb donkey. Kids are not half as discombobulated by this as adults, who understand that the fun is not supposed to be in the hitting but in the breaking. Dumb adults. Finally the fathers move in to tear the thing limb from limb.

—No matter how much you pay a clown to entertain, it could never be enough. Just as you are finally ready to shut all the little guests in the laundry room—"Look, here's a game— fold the towels!"—he has managed to set up his equipment. You have an hour to eat, to breathe, to discover that someone put the bag of malted-milk balls in the dishwasher and then turned it to the pots-and-pans cycle.

—The most important thing to remember about the spacing of your children is not contained in any book. It is that the older one should have a birthday before the younger one. Otherwise you will hear the sentence "But when is it *my* birthday?" spoken in a whine for three or four months on end.

—Everything positive you have ever taught your child will evaporate when the gifts are opened. And I'm not talking about when they are opened at his own party, when he will only remove clothing from the box and toss it over his shoulder. All year long you have been talking about sharing, about waiting your turn, and about not going berserk in public, and suddenly, at another person's birthday party, the child is confronted by an enormous pile of presents, none of which are for him. A chain of ganglia within his little slicked-down head fire off, and he shrieks, "I want them ALL." He is carried into another room, where he is promised gifts on his own birthday if he calms down. No way.

I would like to blame my mother for not teaching me these things, but she did not know them. When she was raising five children there were no piñatas, no clowns. Birthday parties were easy. If your child's birthday fell during the school year, you packed two dozen cupcakes in a box and took them to school, where the child was serenaded with the kid version of "Happy Birthday" at recess. "You look like a monkey/And you smell like one too," everyone sang, breathless with the hilarity of the lyrics; then they ate the icing off the cupcakes and went back to fractions. If your child's birthday fell during the summer, you had a family barbeque at which the only permissible gifts were underwear, socks, or a new missal. My birthday happens to be in July; I always had a sparkler in my cake instead of candles, which was considered the height of sophistication at that time.

Now those wonderful folks who brought you designer sneakers, baby vegetables, and insider trading are giving children's birthday parties, and no one gives missals as gifts. One clown told me, his face grim beneath his painted-on happy face, that he had performed at a party at which the children booed his balloon animals. (I hope all such children will someday be tried as adults rather than juveniles, and given life without parole in the fifth grade.) My own children have not gone to enough parties to get uppity over even the most pathetic balloon animals, but the elder one is pushing it. He wants dinosaurs on his cake. "Not brontosauruses," he says, knowing that I'll opt for the easy outline. "Styracasauruses." Last year he wanted helicopters. At midnight my husband found me leaning over an unmarked expanse of white icing with a tube of blue goo in one hand and an old copy of *Newsweek* with a fairly clear helicopter photograph propped up against a mixing bowl. "I think you're losing it," he said. What did he know? No one ever told his analyst that his father never made him a birthday cake. All he has to do is beat the piñata into submission.

I'm in charge of the cake. It was chocolate. It had Nestlé's Quik in it. (There's a confession for you.) It had buttercream icing. I always make the cake. I feel like it puts me in touch with the elemental aspects of motherhood: that is, I get to lick the bowl. All my childhood, all I ever thought on the day before my birthday was "Someday I will be old enough to make my own cakes and to lick the bowl all by myself." Of course, what I really meant was "Someday I will be old enough to make my own cakes and eat all the batter instead of pouring it into the pan." Unfortunately I reckoned without the children. The older child helped me make the cake for the younger one. At one point, in violation of decent human standards, I found myself wrestling with him over who would lick the spoon. I lost. I will make his cake in the dead of night, while visions of styracasaurus dance in his head, and I will get the spoon and the mixer blades. We are losing the birthday-party wars, but I will win some small battles. Next year, enough wine.

A SECRET LIFE

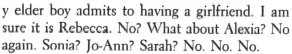

My elder boy admits to having a girlfriend. I am sure it is Rebecca. No? What about Alexia? No again. Sonia? Jo-Ann? Sarah? No. No. No.

"Miss King," he says impatiently, amazed that I could be so dim.

Miss King is his preschool teacher this year. She overcame unbelievable odds to win his heart. The unbelievable odds were the much beloved Mrs. Frank. She was last year's passion. Now she has faded into the glow of fond remembrance.

"What do you like best about Miss King?"

"I can't tell you."

And so his secret life begins.

I remember the first stirrings of my own, when I squirreled away contraband in my desk at school, safe from my mother's eyes (except for the sanitized view offered on parents' night). The power of that secret life, contained as it was in a cheap powder-blue Leatherette diary with a tin key, and the exhilaration: the feeling of being on my own, of hating my bag lunches because they represented a connection, however tenuous, to adults back home. I lobbed the hard-boiled egg on which my mother had painted a picture of a princess into the trash, and bought packaged cupcakes instead.

All over America we children sauntered home at 3:00 P.M. with the same answer to the same question: What did you do in school today? Nothing. The houses that were havens slowly turned into massive invasions of privacy except for the room at the end of the hall with the single bed, the yellow flowered curtains, the bulletin board and the books. My bedroom door had a sign: Keep Out. This Means You! The "i" was dotted with a daisy.

Times have not changed. For weeks, my son and I walked home from school and discussed the new song about the five little snowmen, the alphabet puzzle, the balance bar in the gym. Then, all at once, feeling his strength, knowing that he was beginning to achieve separation, he shut down on me.

"What did you do in school today?" "I can't tell you." At least that is an improvement over "nothing" and its undertones of teachers whiling away the day drinking coffee and reading magazines. "It is my privacy," Quin finally said, hoisting me on my own petard. Privacy is a big word in our house now that I have taught it to my children. The little one has just learned to say it. When you are in the bathroom, he enters and loudly intones "privacy." Then he hangs around, showing that he has gained mimickry but not comprehension.

The older one has not yet invoked the privacy privilege about his room, just the bottom bunk. This is what he has in it: three triangular wooden blocks, an Etch-A-Sketch, a copy of *Babar and His Children* and one of *Mother Goose*, two empty coffee cans, the raggedy red-and-white clown that is his comfort object, a stuffed version of Max in his wolf suit from *Where the Wild Things Are*, three small pillows, a down comforter, and a wire whisk that is well on its way to replacing the clown for reasons I cannot divine. (In the middle of all this, there is usually a little oval empty spot reserved for sleeping.) The last time I changed the sheets he went berserk. "You touched my stuff," he keened, and while my mouth said, "Don't be silly," my brain traveled back to the time my mother cleaned my closet. "You invaded my privacy," I said, eleven years old and disdainful, which is probably redundant.

This is the point, isn't it? I learned at least one thing from the New Testament—that mothers have children to sacrifice them for the greater good. It turns out that this is true, and that the greater good is their independence. But between A and Z lies a minefield of MMMM's. First there is the shock of distance, of realizing that life continues, even when there is no mother to observe it. Later comes the contempt. I remember it well, thinking that needing my parents was a pathetic emotional rag left over from my baby clothes.

When does understanding emerge? I suppose it's different for each of us. The cord lay slack when I was a child; it twisted and pulled and occasionally broke later, when I was running in another direction. Now it is a nice straight line. It would be too much to say that my father and I are living parallel lives, but we are both going the same way. I have my secret life and he has his. Both of us know they are not so wonderful that we have to surround them with so much psychic barbed wire. And now we each know how to back off.

I must nonetheless learn this all over again, now that I must back off in a different direction. My children and I are not going the same way. I know that is necessary, and good. It is sad, though. Quin has a secret life, the first thing he has ever had constructed by and belonging only to him, and each year it will grow. One day he was singing a song I had never heard before. "What is that song?" I asked. "I can't teach it to you," he said. Today, it is can't. Tomorrow, won't. Someday he may teach it to me, but by that time I will already know it. That is the point, isn't it?

I remember lying on the bed when my second child was handed to me, all mottled pink and blue like the wrapping paper at a baby shower; I looked down at the umbilical cord still attached to both our bodies. Then, snip—it begins. Separation. Distance. Perhaps, someday, estrangement. Privacy. Intimacy. Miss King makes better snacks than I do. Ah me.

BABY GEAR

ell, another year has gone by and still the Nobel Prize has not been awarded to the inventors of the Snugli baby carrier. I can't figure it. Here you have someone (I prefer to think that it's a woman) who has come up with an invention that takes literally hundreds of thousands of people who have lost the use of their hands and gives them a new lease on life. They can pick up oranges in the supermarket, they can flip through magazines, they can smear lipstick on the backs of their hands in a test try, and all this despite the fact that they have babies.

That this kind of achievement could go unrecognized is beyond me. The only people who have come close in the circles of civilization in which I currently mingle are the folks who developed the baby backpack and who took young impressionable people who heretofore thought the world consisted of knees, cuffs, and running shoes and enabled them to see at adult eye level. I say bravo.

These are exciting times in which I live. My mother-in-law gasped at her first sight of a collapsible stroller. It was not the miracle of engineering, the sleek design; it was the bittersweet (in that order) memory of pushing perambulators the size of sanitation trucks up steps. My father, who had five children and yet whose experience at holding babies was basically confined to the baptismal font, was mesmerized by the sight of an infant confined to its mother's chest in a blue corduroy Snugli. "They didn't have anything like that when you were kids," he said. Actually they did, but my mother owned the contraption; it was called arms, and it had no warranty and a limited life span.

Consider the snap-crotch T-shirt. It has changed life as I know it. Grown grandmothers, people who will commit physical violence at a good department-store sale, became emotional when they first saw it—in plain white, never mind the little pastel prints. Even the utilitarian Oshkosh overall is a phenomenon, sharing with the snap-crotch T-shirt the ability to cover a baby's great protruding pot in a way hitherto unknown. Finally, babies are losing that sideshow look they had when they wore clothes like ours.

It is my theory that those clothes—the little pants that slipped below the belly, the little shirts that rose above it— were a visible manifestation of the contempt big business secretly had for babies. Babies drool, eat disgusting food, have rarely read anything interesting in the last week, and never buy low and sell high. Today, clothes for babies look different from clothes for adults, which is all to the good. This does not reflect any heightened respect for babies, only an appreciation of our need to pretend we have such heightened respect.

Nevertheless official recognition has lagged. Cynics would suggest that this is because babies have never been a compel-

ling special-interest group, but this belies the fact that most of
the baby inventions of the last two decades were developed not
for babies but for the convenience of adults. (The exception is
the baby backpack, which is convenient only for those adults
who incorporate into their regular weekly workout the lifting
and carrying of twenty pounds of dead weight between their
shoulder blades.) There is the Swyngomatic, which enables
parents to consume enough calories to maintain body weight
and energy. Most babies can tolerate the Swyngomatic for at
least fifteen minutes, which has been shown to be sufficient
time to throw the baby in the swing, wind it up, sit down,
shovel your food in and have that all-important glass of wine
before the baby starts to cry. Some babies are even said to be
entertained by swinging in the Swyngomatic for a full hour at
a time, although no one I know has ever actually met such a
baby.

There is also the Sassy Seat, a freestanding baby seat that
attaches to the end of a table and is held on by the weight of
the child's body within it. Many new parents think the wonderful thing about the Sassy Seat is that it eliminates the need for
a high chair and can be taken anywhere. True, but not most
important. The best thing about Sassy Seats is that grandmothers cannot figure out how they work and are in constant fear
of the child's falling. This often makes them forget to comment on other aspects of the child's development, like why he
is not yet talking or is still wearing diapers. Some grandmothers
will spend an entire meal peering beneath the table and saying,
"Is that thing steady?" rather than, "Have you had a doctor
look at that left hand?" This is clearly more important than
being able to take the seat to a restaurant.

One can only assume that the big boys in Stockholm have
never seen a Sassy Seat or have never had children. How else
to explain their stubborn refusal to honor these phenomena

and their inventors, and their willingness to concentrate instead on biomolecular theory and the cultivation of strange little things in pond scum?

Next year I will lobby again for the Snugli and, failing that, the snap-crotch T-shirt. (I'm sure I am not the only one who has hypothesized that both are a product of the same fertile mind.) In the meantime, I feel a groundswell of support building for those little refastenable tapes on disposable diapers. A mother of four grown children said just the other day that if she had had them, it would have changed her life; it would have erased forever the myriad tiny holes made by diaper pins that she still carries, even today, in the tip of her index finger.

HURT
FEELINGS

The most hateful words I've heard in the last three years were "He'll need surgery." It was not major surgery, thank God; we brought him in early in the morning and carried him out at sunset. But giving anyone permission to open up the blue-white body of your two-year-old is dreadful. I even held him while they administered the anesthesia, a bright idea I pursued with great parental indignation for the sake (allegedly) of the child's psychological well-being, so that he would not be surrounded by strangers.

By the time I had on my white paper moon suit, my surgical mask and my cap, I could have been Lon Chaney for all he knew; that I was helping to hold him down as he struggled didn't seem to diminish the terror in his eyes. The only effect of the exercise was that I had to leave the operating theater, fall against my husband, and burst into tears on his shirt front, my nose running into my disposable mask.

Other parents gasp when they hear this story, and on paper it is probably the worst thing that has happened to my child since he was born, although the three stitches in the palm of his hand last month run a close second. In reality, things like this do not bother me as much as I thought they would. I am pretty good at emergencies, amazingly calm and well-organized considering that I am the sort who never seems able to find two matching shoes in my closet.

So it is only in theory that those things sound like the torments of the damned. It is something else that haunts me about being a mother.

One day I was at the playground with my son, and everywhere there were children just a little older than he, skinny four- and five-year-olds, infinitely inventive giants hanging from the monkey bars and swinging so high the chains strained against their moorings. Time after time he approached them, his hands linked behind his back, and tried—not well—to talk to them, to make friends. Time after time he was ignored, too young to be worthy of notice. Finally, his shoulders slumped and he came back to me, his thumb in his mouth, rebuffed one time too many. I took him home.

Such a small thing, but I can't even think of it without wanting to cry—for the worst things I remember about childhood aren't the physical injuries, the broken nose on the gravel driveway or the bad belly flop off the high board at the local pool. The worst was hurt feelings. When I think of them dispassionately now, they seem so silly, but even as the adult in me is chuckling, from somewhere in the distant past a feeling rises in the gorge, that hot, awful flush and surge in the stomach that comes when you feel ashamed to be yourself.

I don't think it would surprise many women to hear that one of the most vivid memories I have of growing up is intercepting and reading the note that the two cutest boys in my eighth-grade class exchanged, describing me as a carpenter's dream—

flat as a board. Funny, huh? And meaningless now, when I am no longer constructed that way and might not care if I were. So why is it more vivid to me than the day my long longed-for sister was born? And why, of all my relations, can I best evoke a great-uncle who never missed one opportunity, always in company, to make a cutting little comment about my sucking my thumb?

I don't mean to suggest that such things are only done by and to children, but we adults, having successfully flattened out the sharp edges and idiosyncratic little corners of our characters to more generally acceptable configurations, usually are adept at keeping them sub rosa. I still get hurt feelings, sometimes seriously hurt feelings, but I meet them with complicated rationalizations. With children it is more difficult, because it is simpler. "They don't like me," my little boy said, when we got home from the playground.

So while I have learned to live with the two small pink scars left over from his hernia surgery, I cannot bear the thought of the hurt feelings that my son will have to endure before he is old enough to will them away. When someone teases him about sucking his thumb, I turn on them, a virago in running shorts and a T-shirt, defending not only the little boy now but the little girl then. The children who will not want to play with him, the teams he will not make, the girls who will laugh at him at dances—sometimes the stitches don't look so bad.

Occasionally, my husband and I try to torture ourselves, prepare ourselves for the worst by reading each other news stories about terrible things happening to children. But when we're talking about real life, our lives, we come again and again to hurt feelings, to the comments about the braces, the best friend who suddenly wasn't, the droop of the shoulders. Then we turn to our sons and sigh. I occasionally wish them to be the kind of people who don't get hurt feelings; they're not, and I would not truly want them to be. Hurt feelings come because they will walk out to the world, their arms open, their chins up. And somebody will boink them one on the head. It is a wonderful thing, and a terrible one, like seeing your mother standing there while a black rubber mask comes down on your face, knowing she will not leave you, but knowing too that she is helping strangers give you pain.

SIBLING
RIVALRY

T he boys are playing in the back room, a study in brotherly love. The younger one has the fire engine and the older one has the tow truck and although entire minutes have passed, neither has made a grab for the other's toy. The younger one is babbling to himself in pidgin English and the older is singing ceaselessly, tonelessly, as though chanting a mantra. It is not until I move closer to the two of them, toe to toe on the tile floor, that I catch the lyrics to the melody: "Get out of here. Get out of here. Get out of here."

Later the older one will explain that he picked up this particular turn of phrase from me, when I was yelling at one of the dogs. (In a similar phenomenon, he always says "Jesus, Mary, and Joseph" when I apply the brakes of the car hard in traffic.) When I said it to the dogs, I meant it figuratively; how Quin means it is less easily classified. I know, because I know where he is coming from. I have vivid memories of being a small girl reading in a club chair, and of having my brother, a year younger than I, enter the room and interrupt me. An emotion as big and as bang-bang-banging as a second heart would fill my ribs. It was, trust me, pure hatred.

This house is full of sibling rivalry right now, as colorful and ever-present as my children's Lego blocks. The preschool class is full of it, too, filled with three-year-olds in various stages of shell shock because their moms and dads came home in the car one day with a receiving blanket full of turf battles, emotional conflicts, and divided love.

Realization has come slowly for some of them; I think it began one day when the younger one needed me more and I turned to him and said, "You know, Quin, I'm Christopher's mommy, too." The look that passed over his face was the one I imagine usually accompanies the discovery of a dead body in the den: shock, denial, horror. "And Daddy is Christopher's daddy?" he gasped. When I confirmed this he began to cry— wet, sad sobbing.

I cannot remember which of my books described sibling rivalry thus: Imagine that one night your husband comes home and tells you that he has decided to have a second wife. She will be younger than you, cuter than you, and will demand much more of his time and attention. That doesn't mean, however, that he will love you any the less. Covers the down side pretty well, doesn't it?

And yet the down side is not the only one; if it were, "Get out of here" would not have such a sweet little melody. My son loves his brother, who is immensely lovable; at the same time, he dislikes his brother intensely. He wants him to be around, but only sometimes, and only on his terms. He is no different from a lot of us, who have fantasies about the things we want and who are surprised by the realities when we get them. He likes the idea of a brother, but not always the brother himself. When his brother is hurt and helpless, he calls him "my baby."

"I don't want my baby to cry, Mommy," he says, which is the kind of line you get into this business to hear.

But when there is a tussle over the fire engine, his baby develops a name, an identity, a reality that is infuriating. "Christopher," he says then, shaking an index finger as short as a pencil stub in the inflated baby face, "you don't touch my truck, Christopher. O.K.? O.K., CHRISTOPHER?"

He actually likes babies; he even wants to bring one home, the two-month-old brother of his friend Sonia. Eric, he thinks, is perfect: he cannot walk, cannot talk, has no interest in Maurice Sendak books, Lego blocks, the trucks, the sandbox, or any of the other things that make life worth living, includ- ing—especially including—me. One day at Sonia's house he bent over Eric's bassinet to say hello, but what came out instead was a triumphant "You can't catch me!" as he sailed away from him.

His baby can't catch him yet, but it's only a matter of time. Then he will have to make a choice: a partner, an accomplice, an opponent, or, perhaps most likely, a mixture of the three. At some point his fantasy of a brother may dovetail with the reality; mine did when my younger brother, the insufferable little nerd with the Coke-bottle glasses whom I loathed, turned into a good-looking teenage boy who interested my girlfriends, had some interesting boyfriends of his own, and was a first-rate dancer. But it's not as simple as that, either. In his bones now my elder son probably knows the awful, wonderful truth: that he and his brother are yoked together for life, blood of each other's blood, joined as surely as if they were Siamese twins. Whether the yoke is one of friendship or resentment, it will inevitably shadow both their lives. That is certainly something to bear, as good a reason as any to look at someone and wish that he could, impossibly, occasionally, go someplace else.

SESAME
STREET

People sometimes ask: Whom would you like to meet most in the whole world, if your press pass magically opened doors and was not just a meaningless rectangle of laminated plastic with a bad picture of you in one corner? I used to have difficulty answering that question. In the course of my professional duties I have met most of the people I wanted to meet. Some of the famous writers were as smart and enthralling as their books, and some were pompous bores. Some of the famous actors were as smart and enthralling as their roles, and some were pompous bores. Sean Connery is remarkably sexy, although monosyllabic and bald. Barbra Streisand has glorious skin and is much smaller than you would imagine. I don't know how tall Paul Newman is.

Now, however, there is someone I want to meet more than anyone else in the whole world. I want to meet the man who decided some time back, during a week in which the rain stopped so seldom that mothers of toddlers were locking themselves in the bathroom to get away from their kids, that the regularly scheduled children's programs on public television would be preempted in favor of the confirmation hearings for Justice William H. Rehnquist. This decision found kids across America, mine among them, saying of Chief Justice Rehnquist what perhaps has never been adequately expressed about him before: "He not Cookie Monster." Out of the mouths of babes.

It was then I realized that *Sesame Street* is my salvation. It is sometimes difficult for me to believe that a scant three years ago I could not tell the difference between Bert (tall, crabby, fastidious, collects paper clips) and Ernie (short, extroverted, messy, deeply attached to Rubber Duckie). It is equally difficult for me to believe that some program director took the show off the air for even a few days for the sake of the judicial confirmation hearings, which to my mind do not qualify as educational television. Oh Lord, you're saying to yourself, not another piece about letter recognition and reading readiness and exposure to good values and alternate cultures on television. "Hah!" as Oscar the Grouch might say. "Bah!"

Sesame Street is my salvation for two reasons. The first is that on a day when the younger child has tried to drink the bottle of floor wax he found in a childproof cabinet, which is secured with a neat little Danish lock he learned to open just after he learned to roll over, and when the older child has taken the floor wax away from him and poured it on the floor where he supposes it belongs (and where, naturally, the golden retriever has found it and licked it up), *Sesame Street* provides an hour of quiet, sustained concentration. And I do not have to feel as though the high-culture police are going to bang down my door and say, "Television, eh? O.K., boys—lower their S.A.T. scores twenty points apiece."

As a nice corollary to *Sesame Street,* my three-year-old can count to twenty, can identify all and draw some of the alphabet, knows how peanut butter and crayons are made, and understands what adoption means. The younger one has a much expanded vocabulary. His first word was Ernie. He can also say Cookie, Big Bird, Bert, and Grover. On occasion he has attempted, without much success, to say Children's Television Workshop.

The other reason *Sesame Street* is my salvation is that it is written for adults. How else to explain the egomaniacal singing bird named Placido Flamingo? ("That not Placido Flamingo," said my elder child one day, when a promotional spot for the real opera singer was on. "Placido Flamingo is pink.") Or the Miami Mice, J. P. and Tito, with their designer suits and carefully groomed whiskers? How else to explain Ferlinghetti Donizetti, the beatnik poet who performs the rappin' alphabet, or the disco sequence in which Grover wears a white three-piece suit with an open-necked shirt and dances on squares of colored light? What about NTV, the station that regularly features a music video by Nick Normal and the Nikmatics titled "The Letter N"? (Actually, a superior music video is the one of a song by How Now and the Moo Wave, who sold milk on the streets before they made it big.) Or the Cookie Monster number, "Hey, Food," taken directly from the Beatles, or the scene when Oscar learns that the Museum of Trash wants to put his trash can in the Cans Festival?

My children don't understand these allusions, but I do; I'm entertained by them, and on a day when I've read *Pat the Bunny* nineteen times, that's no small thing. I have two theories about how the allusions get in there. Either the people who make *Sesame Street* are looking out for parents' interests, or they are bored out of their gourds counting up to twelve and finding words that begin with the letter b, and so are amusing themselves.

I prefer the latter hypothesis. Certainly, that program director I want so badly to meet was not thinking of parents, an oversight I will force him to confront if we do meet. Of course, that's not all I'll do. I don't want to be more graphic, but if any of you recall what Oscar did to Luis the day he tricked him into looking into the trash can—well that's the kind of thing I have in mind.

THE
SECOND
CHILD

The second child was a year old yesterday. He is everything I wanted to be as a child: fearless, physical, blond. He takes no prisoners. He has also changed my life. Before him, we were two adults and a child they both adored. With him, we are a family. There is no going back.

I had a crisis of confidence when the second child was, quite literally, on the way. We were timing contractions and watching *Bachelor Party* on cable TV when I was felled by the enormity of what we had done. As a textbook-case eldest child—a leader, a doer, a convincing veneer of personality and confidence atop a bottomless pit of insecurity and need—I suspected we were about to shatter the life of the human being we both loved best in the world. We were about to snatch away his solitary splendor. Worse still, to my mind, we were about to make some unsuspecting individual a second child, a person whose baby clothes would be mottled with banana stains the first time he ever wore them, who would have a handful of photographs scattered amidst the painstaking documentation of his brother's life. An also-ran. A runner-up. "This is the heir, and that is the spare," the Duchess of Marlborough once said of her two sons.

The second child came prepared. He had a true knot in his cord, and it was wrapped around him three times, so that he emerged looking like a kidnap victim. It turned out he was feisty and winning, intrusive and alert. His character (not to mention his yellow hair) demanded clothes of his own. He clamored for the camera. He knew what he was doing. More important, so did I. The first child got me shiny new, like a new pair of shoes, but he got the blisters, too. The second child got me worn, yes, but comfortable. I told the first child I would never go away, and lied. I told the second child I would always come back, and spoke the truth. The second child had a mother who knew that the proper response to a crying baby was not to look up "Crying, causes of" in the index of Dr. Spock. As a matter of fact, he had a mother who was too busy to read childcare books at all, and so was in no position to recognize whether his "developmental milestones" were early/ late/all/none of the above.

What had I expected of the first child? Everything. Rocket scientist. Neurosurgeon. Designated hitter. We talked wisely at cocktail parties about the sad mistake our mothers had made in pinning all their hopes and dreams on us. We were full of it.

I have always been a great believer in birth order. I will chat with someone for fifteen minutes and suddenly lunge at them: "You're an oldest child, aren't you?" That means something specific to me, about facing the world and facing yourself. My husband is also an oldest child, and the slogan one of his brothers coined for him is instructive: either pope or president. Not in words but in sentiment, my siblings felt the same about me. A substantial part of my character arises from such expectations.

I worried about that with the second child, worried that the child called Number One would always be so. During my second pregnancy, when I drank a bit of wine and forgot to count my grams of protein, I wondered if I was being more relaxed—or simply careless.

When I went into labor with the first, I sat down and wrote my thoughts in the beginning of his baby book. With the second, I went to a barbecue next door and then put the first to bed. The elder son was born with considerable pain, manhandled into the world with those great silver salad spoons called forceps, and when he was laid in my arms by the nurse, he looked like a stranger to me. The second somersaulted onto the birthing room bed, and as I reached down to lift him to my breast, I said his name: "Hello, Christopher." And as I saw his face, like and yet not like his brother's, I suddenly realized that wine or no wine, he had arrived with a distinct advantage. He came without baggage, after I had gotten over all the nonsense about in-utero exposure to music, and baby massage, and cloth vs. disposable diapers. What a wonderful way to be born.

And so it has occurred to me often in the last year that I must strive to give our elder son some of those things that in the usual course of events come to the younger ones. I worry less now about the second being an also-ran than I do about the first being the kind of rat-race marathon runner that birth order, in part, made me. The saddest thing I always imagined about the second child was that we would have no hopes and dreams for him. I was wrong. What he has taught us is that we will have hopes and dreams, and he will decide whether he is willing to have anything to do with them. I accept him. Perhaps in other times, or with other people, that might mean settling for less. I like to think that in his case it means taking advantage of more.

Perhaps it means that I will not push him when he needs to be pushed. I hope not. And perhaps it means I will push my first child—whose each succeeding year and stage will be inaugurals for me—when I should not do so. One teaches me as we go along, and the other inevitably reaps the benefits of that education. Each child has a different mother—not better, not worse, just different. My greatest hope and dream now is that, taken together, these two ends will make me find a middle ground in myself from which I will be happy to observe them—neither pope nor president nor obsessively striving to be either, but simply two people, their own selves, making allowances for me.

GAY

When he went home last year he realized for the first time that he would be buried there, in the small, gritty industrial town he had loathed for as long as he could remember. He looked out the window of his bedroom and saw the siding on the house next door and knew that he was trapped, as surely as if he had never left for the city. Late one night, before he was to go back to his own apartment, his father tried to have a conversation with him, halting and slow, about drug use and the damage it could do to your body. At that moment he understood that it would be more soothing to his parents to think that he was a heroin addict than that he was a homosexual.

This is part of the story of a friend of a friend of mine. She went to his funeral not too long ago. The funeral home forced the family to pay extra to embalm him. Luckily, the local paper did not need to print the cause of death. His parents' friends did not ask what killed him, and his parents didn't talk about it. He had AIDS. His parents had figured out at the same time that he was dying and that he slept with men. He tried to talk to them about his illness; he didn't want to discuss his homosexuality. That would have been too hard for them all.

Never have the lines between sex and death been so close, the chasm between parent and child so wide. His parents hoped almost until the end that some nice girl would "cure" him. They even hinted broadly that my friend might be that nice girl. After the funeral, as she helped with the dishes in their small kitchen with the window onto the backyard, she lost her temper at the subterfuge and said to his mother: "He was gay. Why is that more terrible than that he is dead?" The mother did not speak, but raised her hands from the soapy water and held them up as though to ward off the words.

I suppose this is true of many parents. For some it is simply that they think homosexuality is against God, against nature, condemns their sons to hell. For others it is something else, more difficult to put into words. It makes their children too different from them. We do not want our children to be too different—so different that they face social disapprobation and ostracism, so different that they die before we do. His parents did not know any homosexuals, or at least they did not believe they did. His parents did not know what homosexuals were like.

They are like us. They are us. Isn't that true? And yet, there is a difference. Perhaps mothers sometimes have an easier time accepting this. After all, they must accept early on that there are profound sexual differences between them and their sons. Fathers think their boys will be basically like them. Sometimes they are. And sometimes, in a way that comes to mean so much, they are not.

I have thought of this a fair amount because I am the mother of sons. I have managed to convince myself that I love my children so much that nothing they could do would turn me against them, or away from them, that nothing would make me take their pictures off the bureau and hide them in a drawer. A friend says I am fooling myself, that I would at least be disappointed and perhaps distressed if, like his, my sons' sexual orientation was not hetero. Maybe he's right. There are some obvious reasons to feel that way. If the incidence of AIDS remains higher among homosexuals than among heterosexuals, it would be one less thing they could die of. If societal prejudices remain constant, it would be one less thing they could be ostracized for.

But this I think I know: I think I could live with having a son who was homosexual. But it would break my heart if he was homosexual and felt that he could not tell me so, felt that I was not the kind of mother who could hear that particular truth. That is a kind of death, too, and it kills both your life with your child and all you have left after the funeral: the relationship that can live on inside you, if you have nurtured it.

In the days following his death, the mother of my friend's friend mourned the fact that she had known little of his life, had not wanted to know. "I spent too much time worrying about what he was," she said. Not who. What. And it turned out that there was not enough time, not with almost daily obituaries of people barely three decades old, dead of a disease she had never heard of when she first wondered about the kind of friends her boy had and why he didn't date more.

It reminded me that often we take our sweet time dealing with the things that we do not like about our children: the marriage we could not accept, the profession we disapproved of, the sexual orientation we may hate and fear. Sometimes we vow that we will never, never accept those things. The stories my friend told me about the illness, the death, the funeral and, especially, about the parents reminded me that sometimes we do not have all the time we think to make our peace with who our children are. It reminded me that "never" can last a long, long time, perhaps much longer than we intended, deep in our hearts, when we first invoked its terrible endless power.

P O W E R

 t two o'clock in the morning I am awakened by the appearance of a person no taller than a fire hydrant, only his black eyes visible over the horizon of the mattress. "What do you want?" I whisper. "Nothing," he whispers back.

What can have woken my younger son and brought him down from the third floor to stand here in his blue pile Dr. Dentons? It usually boils down to some small thing: a glass of water, a night light, a token rearrangement of the blanket. I always suspect that, if he could put it into words, the explanation would be something else entirely: reassurance that he is not alone in a black world, that nothing horrible is going to happen before daybreak, that someday he will sleep the sure, steady, deep sleep that his elder brother sleeps in the twin bed next to his own. His search for reassurance leads him to our bed, where two terribly fallible people toss and turn, the closest thing he knows to God.

This is what no one warns you about, when you decide to have children. There is so much written about the cost and the changes in your way of life, but no one ever tells you that what they are going to hand you in the hospital is power, whether you want it or not.

I suppose they think you know this, having been on the receiving end all your life, but somehow it slipped to the back of my mind. I was the eldest in a large family; I was prepared for much of what having a baby required. I knew how overwhelming were the walks, the feeding, the changing, the constancy of the care. I should have known, but somehow overlooked for a time, that parents become, effortlessly, just by showing up, the most influential totems in the lives of their children.

We have only to study ourselves, our friends, and the world of amateur and professional psychologizing in which we all live to know that parents someday will be cited as the cause of their children's (choose as many as you like): inability to open up, affinity for people who belittle and hurt them, vulnerability, inferiority. Occasionally—very occasionally—their accomplishment and their strength. We need to find our weaknesses outside ourselves, our strength within. I knew that I read *Portnoy's Complaint*, D. H. Lawrence, and Eugene O'Neill. And yet I had managed to depersonalize the message until nights like this one, when I wake up with the moon shining through the window and stare back at a person who, staring at me, seems to be saying, "You are, therefore I am."

I am not comfortable with this, which is a little like saying I don't like having green eyes. "Remember that you are the world to your child," one pamphlet I was given says. Oh, great. After a lifetime of yearning for egalitarian relationships, of trying to eschew power plays with other human beings, I find myself in a relationship which, by its very nature, can never really be equal nor free from a skewed balance of power.

We dwell so often on the harm that can be done by exercising that power malevolently, by those people who hit their children, or have sex with them, or tell them day after day that they are worthless and bad. Free of those things, I am more troubled by the subtleties. Raising children is a spur-of-the-moment, seat-of-the-pants sort of deal, as any parent knows, particularly after an adult child says that his most searing memory consists of an offhand comment in the car on the way to second grade that the parent cannot even dimly recall. Despite what the books suggest, you usually do not have several weeks to puzzle out how to separate battling siblings or what to say about death. So it is inevitable that, after a hard day, I occasionally sit back and think about whether I made any crucial mistakes between the chocolate pudding and the hide-and-go-seek. The answer is probably no. But still I consider the question—of passive power, of the power of suggestion, imitation, reaction.

Perhaps I have been preoccupied with all this lately because, despite the difference in their ages, my sons have dovetailed in a developmental stage and have both fallen in love with me. I can see it in their eyes. For the elder one, this is the grand passion before he lets go, flies off into the male world, switches his identification to his father. For the younger, this is the cleaving to me absolutely which anticipates that process. It is all in the books. Spock says it's fine as long as the child does not become "too close" to the parent of the opposite sex. "In that case, it's wise to get the help of a child guidance clinic," he adds.

There's not much to cure what ails me. I am aghast to find myself in such a position of power over two other people. Their father and I have them in thrall simply by having produced them. We have the power to make them feel good or bad about themselves, which is the greatest power in the world. Ours will not be the only influence, but it is the earliest, the most ubiquitous, and potentially the most pernicious. Lovers and friends will make them blossom and bleed, but they may move on to other lovers and friends. We are the only parents they will have. Sometimes one of them will put silky arms around my neck and stare deep into my eyes like an elfin Svengali and say with full force of the heart, "I love you." The vowel in that middle word dips and lengthens, like a phrase in a Brenda Lee song. My first reaction is to be drowned in happiness. My second is to think: don't mean it so much. Don't feel it so deeply. Don't let me have so much influence over you. Of course, I have no choice. And neither do they.

FOOLING
AROUND

GOSSIP

So I'm reading about Joan Collins, who got married last year in Las Vegas to a man fourteen years her junior whose only résumé description was "former Swedish pop star." And I'm reading about Sylvester Stallone, who married a woman usually photographed wearing no more than the equivalent of a bandanna, who introduced herself by sending a photograph to his hotel room after she had ditched her baby and her first husband in Denmark. (I mean, what are they feeding them in Scandinavia? Human blood?) And I see that these people are getting divorced.

Somehow I am no more surprised than I was to hear that people claiming to be Elvis's love children are sprouting like soybeans all over the South. As the Everly Brothers once said so wisely, love is strange. Particularly when you live in Hollywood.

Lifestyles of the Rich and Predictable—I love them. I read *People* magazine every week, and believe me, I don't read it for those dumb Q and As about how stress can make you sick, or the pieces about the Johnsons, who run the biggest little pig farm in Iowa. I read it for Joan and Stallone and Farrah and Ryan and Tatum and Liz. I love the way these people live, because there's such an incredible logic to it all: love children, the Betty Ford clinic, personal relationships with the spirit world. If you get married in Las Vegas and the groom wears white and carries a simple bouquet of premarital contracts, common sense tells you that a divorce will follow in very short order, and that someone will be represented by Marvin Mitchelson. You know what to expect from Liz Taylor's life. First she shows up at something with a guy. Then she gets some large jewelry from the guy. Then she marries him. Then she divorces him.

Yes, these people lead lives with definition and norms. It's the rest of us who have weird, off-the-wall ways. In my circle it is not totally uncommon for a man to come home one night after fourteen years of marriage, two children, two renovations, three attempts at the Scarsdale diet, a stint at Smokenders, and one midlife crisis, and say, without warning, on a day no better and no worse than thousands of others, "I don't love you. I never loved you. I'm leaving." And there you are, ditched by a person who is not even Scandinavian, with no jewelry, and no premarital contract, hit up side of the head.

In Hollywood, I am sure you would expect this. Your husband would open his mouth and before he got a word out you could just say, "I'm not stupid. I saw in the *Star* while I was in the supermarket line that Priscilla is having your love child."

My husband is appalled—not by Joan's ex-husband's little passionflower or those wild accusations about Sly's estranged wife and her secretary, but by the fact that I am interested in it all. He's even threatened that if I abdicate my responsibilities and order too much Chinese takeout he's going to tell the world that I can't get going in the morning without a cup of

coffee and a gossip column. Let him. Where else am I going
to get this stuff? Here at home? This is not a life that is going
to wind up in the full-color tabloids, no matter how you cut it.
"Quin and Christopher in Backyard Wading Pool—AS
YOU'VE NEVER SEEN THEM BEFORE!" "Gerry: There
Were Never Enough Clean Socks." "Love on the Rocks: Bot-
tled Salad Dressing the Last Straw." Circulation plummets.

The appeal of these people is that they are not at all what
I find at home. (For one thing, they decorate in all-white.) It's
a great combination—glamour and predictability. We're not
strong on either one of them around here. My kids might turn
out to be architects, or heavy metal drummers (please, God,
no), or farmers, or lawyers. They may be good or bad or good
and bad. This is different from the kids of celebs, who are
either very, very good ("LISA MARIE PRESLEY: 'I'll never
be like my father.' ") or very, very bad (LISA MARIE: 'She's
just like Elvis,' says Priscilla.").

My friends don't have glamorous predictable lives, either;
they have to make do with their relationships instead of figur-
ing they'll meet someone better on the set of their next film.

Maybe I'd be more tolerant of, say, the Princess of Wales's
problems if she was a friend of mine. She might call and say,
"He's too old, he's never home, all he wants to do is garden
and go to swamis, his mother thinks she runs the world." And
I would tell her, "Look, Diana, he's a great father, he never
embarrasses you in public, he wears nice clothes, and he keeps
the garden looking great. Plus you have a terrific house and
great jewelry, and anyhow, when was the last time I met Rod
Stewart or Timothy Dalton?"

Whereas when I read about her in the tabloids (DI DISGRUN-
TLED, DANCES AT DISCO) I just think, "It'll never last. And
anyhow, what did she expect?" She should have known that
there are standards in the public eye. I've learned them just by
keeping tabs on the divorce courts and the columns.

Let's say Sly calls me up and says, "I met this girl. She's seventeen years younger than I am, six feet tall, and she's usually sort of seminude and draped all over me. Her acting credits could fill a matchbook, but I'm going to put her in my next movie, and also marry her." What could you say, except: Get a premarital agreement and insist on having *People* shoot you on your good side when the separation is announced.

THE
PAINTERS

The painters. Don't the very words strike fear into your heart? We've all seen it happen. A colleague comes into the office. His hair is standing on end, his tie is awry, and there is a pale swipe of primer on the cuff of his pants leg. He collapses at his desk. "How about a drink?" he says hopefully. "It's ten o'clock in the morning," you reply, and suddenly you know.

The painters. There's the Stephen King megaseller that would scare the overalls off me. *Dropcloth.* Woo.

The painters are going into their fifth week at our house, which is right on schedule, according to painter time, because they said they would be done in two. "There was a lot more work than we expected," said the lead man, his hair prematurely white from plaster dust and homeowners. Why don't they just have that line printed on their business cards? That and "We'll just sheetrock it over"? I, for one, would not hire a painter who did not say at least once that they would just sheetrock it over. How much experience could he possibly have? Would he know to direct the entire team to leave their coffee containers and their Fritos bags on the floors to attract roaches? Would he know to paint the windows shut except for the window in the master bath, which must be painted open? Would he be the kind of guy who would get spackle in the sugar bowl? Would he charge enough, enough so that when I see a woman at the supermarket driving a Mercedes convertible and wearing a fun fur, I know without doubt that it is his wife?

Painters may think I am picking on them. I can only reply: it's about time. Of course, they're not alone. Think about the plumbers, for example, if it's late afternoon and you can handle a major brainstorm. Perhaps we share the same one. He's the guy who arrives and says "There's nothing wrong with this furnace." Except that it does not provide what we in the rank and file refer to as heat. "I can understand that that's a problem for you, but there's nothing wrong with this furnace." The roofers are pretty terrific, too. I once had a roofer come down my fire escape and tell me he believed with all his heart that my roof was terminal. And I had an entire house, actually occupied by furniture, dependent on that roof. It makes you wonder why your place has a door. Why not just a huge yawning pit of a mouth, red, with teeth, that every once in a while bellows FEED ME MONEY!!

But somehow the painters are the worst. Maybe it's because you remember them long after they are gone, when you can feel the grit of the plaster dust in your mouth and you're actually grateful for it because you can't afford groceries anyway. I once had painters I thought I could trust. It was in New York City, where I had an apartment the size of a luxury car. I hired painters to paint it, although by law my landlord was obliged to have it painted every millennium or so. This is a funny joke in New York, a frequent subject of cocktail party conversation and topical cartoons, because if painting is handled by your landlord, this is how it works: the painters arrive. They mix three cupfuls of white paint with a bathtub full of water. Then they throw it at the wall. Anything that drips to the floor counts as painting the molding. Then they stand at the door and bid you adieu for an extremely long time, usually longer than they spent painting. Then you hire real painters.

The painters I hired were feminist painters. That was their angle. There were three of them and we had a cordial conversation about the politics of the color peach for a bedroom (was it a capitulation to traditional female sex roles? Did it indicate a lack of commitment? Would it wind up looking pink?) before they began to spackle up a storm. They were excellent plasterers and painters, and when they were finished they gave me a bill so large that recently, some ten years after the event, I hypothesized that their contribution alone may have played a major role in the lobbying effort against Justice Bork. Friends thought I was looking a gift painter in the can. "You had a white couch and you still have a white couch," one said. "Do you have any idea how rare that is?"

I guess they broke me in. I am reconciled to painters now. I understand their language. "It will look great" means "you will learn to live with it." "We've got a problem with this spot" means "there will be a large mound on the wall." Recently I was on a business trip to a country roughly five thousand miles from my home, and when I called, my husband informed me that the stock market had crashed and the painters had nicked a plumbing pipe in the wall. "Listen to me," I said slowly and distinctly. "This is very important. Did you personally witness a nicked pipe or did the painters tell you they nicked the pipe?"

"Why is that important?" my husband said.

"Because if the painters told you they nicked a pipe what

that means is that they ripped every inch of plumbing out of the house and threw the bathtubs out the windows onto the lawn."

Long silence. "Why did we need the house painted?" said my husband, who will always go for the jugular.

"It is God's way of cutting us down to size."

"Aren't you interested in the market," he added.

"Did we lose any money?" I asked.

"No, but the painter did. He says he took a real bath on his blue chips and he won't be able to finish the dining room."

"How about a drink?" I asked my husband.

"It's ten o'clock in the morning," he said.

"Not where I am," I replied, pouring the vodka and tossing my color chips into the trash.

HEMLINES

see short skirts are coming back. This should make my husband happy. The first time he met me, I was wearing a skirt so short that if I had reached for something on a closet shelf it would have constituted a crime in some states. My hair was almost as long as my dress. In the years since, the trend toward shorter hair and longer skirts has often filled him with a deep sadness. He believes that women should show lots of leg and no ear.

I am of two minds. I love short skirts, although I have always had the traditional Irish girl piano legs, suitable for field hockey but not for display. But I feel as if I'm a little too something now to show my legs: too grown-up, too married and motherly, too old. Was it in an Agatha Christie mystery that the detective figured out a suspect was lying about her age by the condition of her knees? I'm haunted by that concept.

I wish this was about what I wear, but in truth

it is about who I am, or at least who I want to appear to be. A friend of mine found herself adrift recently in a department store, wandering amid the racks in some distress. She finally had the money, but she didn't have the self-image. A simple shopping trip had turned existential. For years she had been one kind of woman, but now she had become another. Who was this person she was attempting to outfit? And was that person a good candidate for knits?

I know just how she felt. Each month the catalogues come and I pick things out: clothes I would have worn ten years ago, clothes I think I should want to wear today, clothes for the collected person that I've always wanted to be. (I am waiting for the catalogue for the person I fear I have become. "Chaos," it would be called. "For the woman who can never find any-thing clean in her bureau drawers.") My closet has a dozen personas lurking inside: shoulder pads, little prints, pleated pants, pleated skirts, fuchsia, black, navy blue. The worst part about cleaning it is chucking unsuccessful past lives: the care-free peasant, the funky girl-about-town, the dress-for-success suits that for one brief horrible period of insecurity and ambi-tion I affected. You cannot give those suits away. You must drive a silver stake through their lapels.

I was a girl who spent ten years of her life wearing a forest-green blazer with a school insignia on the breast pocket, a plaid pleated skirt and saddle shoes, so I suppose I shouldn't com-plain. Better this than my mother's closet, filled with her own little uniforms: the nice suit with the shell blouse and matching pumps and purse for card parties, the pastel shirtwaist dress with Peter Pan collar and pleated front for dinner, the madras Bermudas and blouse for the backyard. The role defined the clothes. Betty Friedan wrote in *The Feminine Mystique* that the question for those times was "Is this all?" Now, of course, we feel differently. I hope this *is* all, because I can't handle any more: so many roles, so many clothes.

I know there are people who will contend that how you look has nothing to do with who you are. There has been a recent exchange of letters about this in Dear Abby; a young woman who wears nothing but garments made of black leather wrote to complain that men got the wrong idea from her personal style. To this Abby replied in essence—and I'm with her all the way on this one—"Get real."

Clothes are some kind of a mirror of what's inside; otherwise, why would maternity dresses be designed to make you look like a baby? A Mohawk is a statement about how you perceive the universe. But young people make these kinds of mistakes unthinkingly. At a dinner several years ago, I ran into a politician I have known for ages. I was wearing my black dinner suit and so was he, and he began to reminisce to a group of people about the first time we had met. It was at a press conference at City Hall—my first press conference, my first visit to City Hall. I was so eager, he said, I appeared to be on drugs. I was so intimidated, he said, that I introduced myself twice to a minor functionary and then stuck to him like glue. And I was wearing hot pants, he said. Have you ever seen an entire decade's worth of credibility crumble before your very eyes? Not pretty.

Now, of course, hot pants have returned to their former status as a condition rather than a garment, and I have developed a bit more sense. But still I feel that I have not got the self-image down, what one of my friends calls "The Look." Now that I have passed from college to first job to marriage to other jobs to kids, I should have some sense of what to take off the rack: Silk dresses? Black separates? Stone-washed denim? It's not that I should know how to dress; I should know who I'm dressing. But when I group my clothing according to the traits conveyed, my closet looks like a convention of multiple-personality cases.

So I contemplate short skirts. They were once me, although

that was a time in my life when my character was so ambiguous it could have qualified as protoplasm. But are they me now? And which me are they? And is that the me I want other people to see? Boy, I wish buying clothes was about clothes. I hate character analysis in front of a three-way mirror, especially when I am looking at the back reflection. I hold up a skirt on a hanger and imagine it ten years from now, a sociological find, a conversation piece: Remember when they tried to bring short skirts back, and you were dumb enough to buy one? Was that really YOU who did that?

SHOP
LIKE
A
MOM

was doing the family grocery shopping accompanied by two children, an event I hope to see included in the Olympics in the near future. Not until we were putting the food on the little treadmill at the checkout counter did I realize I had not personally picked out many of the items in the cart.

There was shoestring licorice, a small jar of macadamia nuts that was more expensive than the earrings I was wearing, and a box of Mallomars. There were also two more boxes of breakfast cereal than I had bargained for: one kind of cereal shaped like tiny ice cream cones filled with chocolate-chip ice cream, and another called Cocoa Puffs, which I remember fondly from my childhood chiefly because they turned the milk brown.

I took all this stuff back amid wild wailing and picked up the mouthful of yogurt raisins my younger child had spit all over the checkout line in his anger and distress. "I shall not be moved," I said in the car, looking at them both in the rearview mirror. "I wanted the ice cream cereal," screamed the elder.

I'm under a lot of pressure to shop like a mom. My mom shopped like a mom, too, but in her day it was easier. Those were the days when people believed that fats were what God put in food to make it taste good. When my mom went shopping, she bought cookies with ingredients that sounded like a science fair experiment, fruit drinks with no fruit, and huge loaves of bread that could be compressed to the size of a handball with one squeeze. It was never enough. There were still the fights with the kids, the incredible outrage we could summon at the suggestion that a four-pound Almond Joy bar was an unreasonable purchase.

Now that I am on the other side, I can understand why a civilized woman who knows the difference between emulsifiers and real food would nonetheless shop like a mom. You want to minimize the fights and you want some appropriate food on hand if by chance you sink to the lowest levels of human degradation and start watching *The Colbys*.

I swore it would never come to this. On the subject of feeding my first child, I was what you might call a real pain. For the first six months of his life he got nothing but breast milk, accompanied by the occasional rhapsody about nourishing him from my own body. When I put him on solids, I carried a little food mill everywhere; it became traditional at family gatherings to see me hunched over a plate of steamed carrots, grinding them and mixing them with yogurt.

I knew those days were gone forever when I found myself recently splitting a bag of Cheez Doodles with my sons. (You know everything about Cheez Doodles by the way Cheez is spelled. I mean, would you buy a sauce for your asparagus called Holl-N-Daze?) It was not companionable; none of us were talking, just scarfing down those little curlicues like attack dogs at feeding time. Finally my first child, he of the breast milk and puréed carrots, looked up and grinned, a salty orange grin. "Mommy, I like this stuff," he said.

The father of the children is disturbed by these lapses. He does not like to come home and, reading the hieroglyphics on their dinner plates, discover that the children ate takeout Chinese food instead of roast chicken and steamed string beans. But the father of the children is not home to hear the pleading: "Please can we have dumplings? Please can we have choo choo pork? Please can we have fortune cookies?" The younger one— who takes after Sylvester Stallone and tends to confine himself to one-word sentences that sound like depth charges detonating—stomps about and shouts, "Spareribs!"

The father of the children remembers a time when I was a careful shopper and a devoted cook. He forgets that at the time my Tupperware was not being used as bathtub toys, my vegetable steamer basket had not become a pond for the plastic dinosaurs, and nobody was using the garlic press as a gun. (It was also a time when I sublimated my true nature and pretended that I thought Ring Dings were revolting, which is a lie.)

The eldest child came home the other day begging, pleading, whining for some fabulous, delicious, absolutely transcendent food he'd had at a friend's house. It was red, he said. It had bananas; you could hold it in your hand and see through to your finger, you could make it dance. We had to have it. With horror I realized what he was saying. He wanted Jell-O.

Do you know that I once had a theory that if you fed children nothing but nutritious foods, with no additives, preservatives, or sugar, they would learn to prefer those foods? I should have recognized the reality at the first birthday party, when tradition triumphed over nutrition and I made chocolate cake for the guest of honor. He put one fistful in his mouth and gave me a look I would not see again until I brought a baby home from the hospital and told him the baby was going to stay. The cake look, roughly translated, said, "You've been holding out on me." He set about catching up. The barber gave him lollipops, the dry cleaner a Tootsie Roll. At the circus he had cotton candy, which is the part of the balance of nature designed to offset wheat germ.

The other night for dinner he was having vegetable lasagna and garlic bread, picking out the zucchini, the spinach, even the parsley—"all the green stuff"—and eating only the parts of the bread that had butter. "Know what my favorite food is, Mom?" he said. "Sugar."

THE
ROYAL
WEDDING
PIG - OUT

T he Royal Wedding Pig-Out began promptly at
5:30 A.M. with the traditional opening of the bag
of peanut M & M's. These were the same peanut
M & M's that were served on this very same sofa
bed at the wedding of Lady Diana Spencer and
the Prince of Wales some years ago (well, not the
same bag, but the same size and variety of candy),
and were in no way meant to reflect on the eating
habits of the bride, the former Miss Sarah Ferguson. It's bad enough having showers and fittings
and rehearsals before your wedding without having everyone talking about how much you weigh.

Several weeks ago, the paper printed the extraordinary measurements of Miss Ferguson,
who is built like a real person who actually con-
sumes food; reporters even slipped a tape around
the hips of her wax facsimile at Madame Tussaud's in London. If she had not become a public
figure the moment Prince Andrew popped the
question, I think Miss Ferguson would have had

an excellent lawsuit on the Tussaud incident alone, something along the lines of first-degree humiliation or conspiracy to commit embarrassment.

The Royal Wedding Pig-Out is an object of ridicule in my home. I will agree to rise before the sun for three special occasions: the ritual feeding of a baby (intermittently), the ritual fishing with the father (very intermittently) and the Royal Wedding Pig-Out (every five years or so). Despite the sporadic nature of the Pig-Out, the rules are clear. There will be tears during the reciting of the vows. The bride will be admired. And the Nestlé Crunch bar will not be eaten until the ceremony is over.

My husband thinks that the Pig-Out is a function of two things: the fact that I am an Anglophile, thanks in part to a profound and very early attachment to the writings of Charles Dickens and good toffee, and the fact that I am a glutton and seek excuses to eat junior high school food. This is accurate but incomplete. I am also a brideophile. On Sundays I read the society announcements. "Bad veil," I mutter while my husband rolls his eyes. I have old scrapbooks filled with photographs of wedding gowns, which I apparently thought, at age thirteen, were the ultimate dress-for-success outfits.

I have outgrown some of my illusions; I no longer think that the Empire waist is attractive, for example. But I still love the idea of women caught in the act of getting married. I could care less about men. When the groom is riding through the streets during the Royal Wedding Pig-Out, I go to the kitchen, make a pot of coffee, and call friends who are Pigging-Out in their own homes and scream, "Is this great or what?"

I have traced this to a time in my life when the sole important occasion with a woman at its center was a wedding. I would gladly stay up all night to see the investiture of Pope Mary I, but the chances of this happening in my lifetime seem slim. I would even go to Washington, which is saying something for me, just to glimpse Jane Q. Public being sworn in as the first female President of the United States, while her husband holds the Bible and wears a silly pillbox hat and matching coat. But for most of my life the only ceremonies I've been to at which women were the stars were weddings. So I like weddings.

This does not necessarily reflect my views on marriage. There are good marriages and bad marriages, but there are no bad weddings, except for those in scuba gear or on horseback. Most weddings have a kind of certainty to them. When I turned on the news last weekend to check out Caroline Kennedy's wedding dress, it was soothing to see that she was as skinny as she was ever going to be in her life, which seems to be the norm for all brides except the current Princess of Wales. It was also reassuring to see that Caroline Kennedy's mother, the most poised woman in America, was in possession of a quivering lower lip.

Sarah Ferguson looked beautiful, too, and she and the bridegroom actually looked like they were in love. (Of course, there are surprises at every wedding. At this one, for example, the Queen wore a creditable hat.) I always feel myself empathizing with the bride. Did she get any sleep? Has anyone mentioned that her necklace is crooked? Doesn't that train weigh a ton? All this once made me think that I would love being the bride myself. That I didn't was one of the two great disappointments of my own wedding. (The other was that my hair did not curl, but that's an ugly story and better forgotten.) Doing it yourself is simply not the same as sitting back with a good candy bar and watching someone else do it, which I suppose is why some people are voyeurs.

I hope Sarah enjoyed herself as much as I did, but I doubt it. She was probably too busy worrying about her veil and her train and whether anyone was going to slip behind her and throw a tape measure around her waist. Now she can relax, eat all she wants, and settle down to the business of being married, which is often more fun than getting married and can be done in much more comfortable clothes.

As for me, I will wait five years for Prince Edward to get married. I've got the Pig-Out down to a science, as precise as the parade route from Westminister Abbey to Buckingham Palace. When they come out on the balcony, I break out the Pepperidge Farm cookies. If, however, there is ever a royal wedding in the late afternoon, Greenwich Mean Time, I have already decided to introduce a Blimpie and a beer.

A
BASEBALL
WIMP

t was during the thirteenth inning, with it all tied up at 3-3, that I found myself hanging over the partition inside a Checker cab, my back end in the back seat, my front end in the front, twisting the dials of the radio to find the playoff game between the Mets and the Astros. My driver, who had been tuned to so-called easy-listening music, was a Thai immigrant who seemed to think that what he was witnessing was exactly what you could expect of indigenous Americans. His English was spotty, but moments before I finally picked up the game amid a ribbon of relentless static, he did manage to say feelingly, "You big fan."

Well, no. Actually, I am what is known in the vernacular as a baseball wimp. I ignore the whole season until, each year at this time, during the playoffs and the World Series, I become terribly interested in baseball. You've heard Reggie Jackson called Mr. October? I am Ms. October.

Someone very nicely described it the other night as eating the
whipped cream off the sundae. At home, not nicely at all, I am
described as a disgrace to a noble sport, a fair-weather fan, a
Joanie-come-lately.

I've always liked baseball, even as a child, when tradition
dictated that I should be prohibited from playing, and my
three brothers should be egged on. I like the sense of both the
camaraderie and the aloneness of it, the idea of nine men
working together in a kind of grand pavane—pitcher to
catcher, shortstop to second baseman to first baseman—and
the idea of one man looking down the loaded barrel of a
pitcher's arm and feeling the nice clean solid thunk as he hits
a ball that will fly into the bleachers. (I like basketball, too. I
do not like football, which I think of as a game in which two
tractors approach each other from opposite directions and col-
lide. Besides, I have contempt for a game in which players have
to wear so much equipment. Men play basketball in their
underwear, which seems just right to me.)

But I like other things, too. I like a sense of drama, and I
have to admit that I just don't find the question of whether
someone is out at the plate in the third inning of the forty-
eighth game of the season that inherently dramatic. I like a
sense of continuity, and in today's baseball you don't get much.
As soon as I take a shine to a player, he's gone—to another
team or to run a car dealership somewhere in the Middle West.
I have never fully recovered from the disappearance of a player
from the Yankees called Chicken Stanley, for whom I developed an unwarranted affection some years back, not because of
his playing or even his funny name, but because he looked
somehow vulnerable and pathetic in pinstripes.

I like a sense of community, and in the early months of the
baseball season it always seems to me that the community
consists mainly of solitary men staring glassy-eyed at television
sets and occasionally saying to befuddled three-year-olds,

"Shortstop! That's a good position for you. Shortstop!" On the occasions when I try to join this community, I always blow it by doing something stupid, like screaming when Reggie Jackson hits a triple because I still think he plays for New York, or saying, when a player comes up to bat, "Boy, he's cute," which can throw a pall on the whole afternoon. Playoff games produce real community. I monitored the final National League playoff game in stages: first with an entire office full of people clustered around a television in midtown Manhattan; then in the cab with the radio; next in a commuter bus in which two people were listening to Walkman radios and reporting to all assembled, saying things like "They've tied it up" (groans) and "The Astros just struck out" (cheers), and then to a street being patrolled by a man in a white Pinto who kept leaning out and yelling, "Top of the sixteenth, still tied." I made it home to watch the last inning with my husband.

Baseball at this stage of the game offers just about everything I want. With only a handful of teams in contention, I can keep track of who's who and what they do best, of who can't run and who can't hit and who can't field. Each play is fraught with meaning, each loss a joy or a disaster. And each game is played before great communities of people, in bars, in rec rooms, even in offices, the ranks of the faithful swelled by those who have a passing interest and those who have no interest at all in baseball, but know a good cliffhanger when they see one—the same kind of people who watched the first episode this season of *Dallas* to see what happened to Bobby and then forgot about it. In fact, at this time of year baseball becomes a different kind of spectacle for me, something more along the lines of *As the Bat Swings*. Will Keith lose his temper? Will Lenny be a hero? Will Davey show emotion? Now we get down to the soap operas, and Chicken Stanley or no Chicken Stanley, I love soap operas.

STUFFING

This is the story of a turkey, and the things she cooked for Thanksgiving dinner. It is not an easy story to tell. It includes a bulb baster, those useless little metal rods Julia Child uses for trussing, and quantities of cheesecloth heretofore undreamed of. And butter—my God, the butter. Even now, a full year later, I can see my hands stretched before me, gleaming horribly like that cranberry jelly you get in a can.

It's hard to know where to begin. My husband says that I was conscious and not on drugs, alcohol, or cold medication when I decided to invite both my family and his family to our home for Thanksgiving dinner last year. Only eighteen people could make it. Some had other commitments. Perhaps they had heard that it would be my first turkey.

I bought the bird from the butcher. "I need the biggest fresh turkey you can manage to trot out," I said, struggling into my competent person's air like a pair of 501 Levi's two sizes too small. The butcher wrote on a piece of brown paper. I went home and read cookbooks. One said that in cooking turkey, allow fifteen minutes a pound. Another said allow twenty-five minutes a pound. One said to cook the turkey five hours. Another said to cook the turkey eight hours. "It depends," said my mother-in-law. "On what?" "On how accurate your oven temperature is," she said.

I was doomed.

"I make a mean duck with orange-cranberry relish," I said hopefully to my husband at breakfast.

"Not on Thanksgiving you don't," he said without looking up from his newspaper.

I knew that there were turkeys available shot full of some stuff that made them all plump and juicy, turkeys that came with little slimy instruction booklets packed in with the giblets, turkeys that even had those plastic daggers that pop up to tell you when they're done. I couldn't buy one of those turkeys because I had long ago sworn off that kind of prepared foodstuff (although on nights when my husband had to work late and the kids were safely tucked away in bed, I would sometimes make myself a big portion of Kraft macaroni and cheese, for old time's sake). I needed a fresh turkey, with no additives, no preservatives, no chemicals, nothing to protect me from the possibility that I would pull something from the oven with white meat resembling wallboard.

It's important to note here what I think of as Quindlen's dictum: It is impossible to cook badly something you love. I am constitutionally incapable of making bad fudge or bad fettuccine Alfredo. I do not love turkey; I don't even like turkey. The only part I eat is the big triangular piece of skin covering the stuffing at the back. My brother-in-law and I have for years bickered over it, although now that we both have children we've gotten pretty adult about the whole thing. We split it and then bicker over who gets the bigger piece. As far as I'm concerned, the rest of the turkey is a testimonial to what boring people we've turned the Pilgrims into. Calvin Trillin is leading a nationwide campaign to have spaghetti carbonara declared the official Thanksgiving food. I say, "Hear, hear!"

That said, the turkey was delivered on Wednesday afternoon. "I hope it fits in your oven," said the butcher, with what I can only describe as a smile. The turkey was enormous. It was as ugly as a baby just after birth and looked about the same: wrinkled, misshapen, with odd bumps and bruises and a weird white-pink color. Luckily, it fit in my oven. It did not, however, fit in my refrigerator.

I was doomed.

"Put it on the fire escape," a friend of mine said, "it's colder out there today than it is in your refrigerator."

"Stray cats," I said.

"Wrap it in foil and put it in a box."

"Rain."

"Put a tarp over it."

"You think of everything," I said. "You come over here and cook this thing."

Well, I did put it on the fire escape, at least until I could farm out all the other food in the refrigerator to my friends. In the morning I put it in the oven. First I stuffed it, rubbed two sticks of soft butter into its pathetic skin and shrouded it in cheesecloth. I worked out a roasting time between five hours and eight hours, basted it every half hour and hoped for the best.

Inevitably, my mind kept turning to the time I first made a chicken, which sounds soothing but wasn't. I was seventeen. My mother talked me through it: season, truss, roast, let rest, carve. The only thing she left out was thaw. Even today, when family members have had a little eggnog and want a good laugh, someone says, "Anna's chicken!" and they all roar and roll around while I have another drink.

I was doomed.

Or so I thought. It was a good turkey; not a great turkey, but not a "family joke" turkey either. It was pretty juicy, and it wasn't raw, and it looks good in the photographs, which is more than you can say for me. The only complaint I have about the whole episode is that I was so busy worrying about the turkey that my brother-in-law got a much bigger piece of skin than I did, which I can assure you will not happen this year. Oh, yes, I'm doing it again this Thanksgiving, making my second turkey for only eleven people. A lot of the others say that since they were here last year, they have to go to the in-laws this year. None of them know about the fire escape, so maybe they are telling the truth.

SILLY

ne of the first terms of art you learn in the newspaper business is something called the silly season, which once upon a time occurred around August. It was that time of the year when news had ground to a dead halt, when the mayor was at the beach, the kids were out of school, and public relations people called up promoting things like the Madonna lookalike contest or the first annual dog Frisbee competition. After Labor Day the pace was expected to quicken again: legislation, Supreme Court decisions, heat complaints, and the press of daily business.

But what many of us began to notice over the years—and what some of you may have noticed, too—is that the silly season has proliferated. Perhaps this has something to do with holiday weekends, which have spread out faster than chicken pox in a first grade class. There's a silly season now that stretches from Thanksgiving to New Year, and another one in May, which is usually linked to spring fever. Slowly but surely, the United States has developed an unbelievable year-round case of senioritis.

I've come to believe that this is because the United States is the silliest nation on the face of the earth, although it probably gets a bit of competition from England, which is silly only because it is so terribly serious. I don't get the impression that the French or the Germans are silly. The Soviets are not silly at all. But this is some silly country we live in, between the bakeoffs and the baby beauty contests and all those events in which people balance pancakes on their noses or bet on which box turtle will cross the finish line first. I believe that Gary Hart had his finger on the American pulse and realized that reentering the presidential race was so silly that Americans just might be amused by it. (I am not saying the United States is a stupid country. Which is why I believe the bumper crop of Gary Hart cartoons, apocryphal stories, and even knock-knock jokes will bear no relation to votes. Since Gary Hart went on *Nightline* and appeared to confuse having female friends with taking yacht trips with actress/models, it is no surprise that he can also confuse amusement with forgiveness.)

My husband and I are educated people, and I can't tell you what a whoop we got out of it when we heard the story— untrue, it developed—that Joe Biden would get back in the race, too. Was that silly or what? "Ted Kennedy's next!" we both shouted. "Nixon," I screamed. "Like the T-shirt says, he's tanned, rested, and ready."

This is very undignified and if I were a serious commentator I would here decry such silliness. But I won't. I was raised in the silly branch of a funny family, and I now help run a silly household myself. My grandfather always played a song on the piano that we called "The Laughing Song." The melody was really only a series of fancy-dancy scales, and there were no lyrics. Instead, along with the syncopated melody, you sang laughter, something like this: ha ha ha ha ha ha ha, ho ho ho ho ho. That was it. The thing about it was, after a few bars somebody would inevitably crack up. Then somebody else, and somebody else again. By the time "The Laughing Song" was over, most of the people in the room would be howling along with it.

That's the kind of environment I grew up in. My father is a very silly man who will do almost anything for a good laugh, although unlike Gary Hart he disdains a cheap one. For a time, we lived amidst the mountains of West Virginia, where the most talked-about programming on the radio was the WWVA Jamboree. And my father would take me with him in the car to the highest elevation in town late at night and fiddle with the car radio dials as delicately as a safe cracker until he picked up Jean Shepherd's monologues. Then we would listen and laugh. I still think my father has never been prouder of me than the day when, accompanying a group of his colleagues to a business lunch, I successfully completed the second anecdote in a two-part joke which required complicity and excellent timing. (My father did think that I should have waited until dessert rather than the main course for my part, but it was a small complaint.)

I don't mean to suggest that we were a whoopee cushion family, the kind who balanced buckets of water over the kitchen door and collapsed into laughter when someone got soaked, although I'd be willing to give that a try. Rather the contrary. Everyone always considered it quite amusing that my grandfather, safely at home, would from time to time send motel postcards which always said "Having a wonderful time. Wish you were here. (Wish I was, too.)" When I was at boarding school my father would habitually send me letters signed Joe, which is not his name. (Today he frequently sends me letters signed "Your husband's father-in-law.") My friends thought this was uproarious, and envied me. I really hated it. No one thinks anything silly is suitable when they are an adolescent. Such an enormous share of their own behavior is silly that they lose all proper perspective on silliness, like a baker who is nauseated by the sight of his own éclairs. This provides another good argument for the emerging theory that the best use of cryogenics is to freeze all human beings when they are between the ages of twelve and nineteen.

I cannot help but feel now that my parents raised me right. Being silly seems the easiest, certainly the most pleasurable way to survive and thrive in these times, particularly during an election year. If I had not been silly I never would have covered the weeklong attempt to inflate a balloon facsimile of King Kong atop the Empire State Building or the invasion of the khapra beetle in lower Manhattan. Silliness has made my life easier. It has certainly made it easier for me to have children. You cannot imagine how much easier it is to have two children under the age of four if you are not only able but willing to do lifelike monkey imitations. This would not be in keeping with a role as a serious commentator, but then there are lots and lots of serious commentators around. And precious few silly ones. Not to mention first-rate monkey impersonators.

KEEPING THE FAITH

I
AM A
CATHOLIC

ominus vobiscum. Et cum spiritu tuo. These are my bona fides: a word, a phrase, a sentence in a language no one speaks anymore. *Kyrie eleison. Confiteor dei.* I am a Catholic. Once at a nursing home for retired clergy, I ate lunch with a ninety-year-old priest, a man who still muttered the Latin throughout the English Mass and ate fish on Fridays. When he learned how old I was, he said with some satisfaction, "You were a Catholic when being a Catholic still meant something."

What does it mean now? For myself, I cannot truly say. Since the issue became material to me, I have not followed the church's teaching on birth control. I disagree with its stand on abortion. I believe its resistance to the ordination of women as priests is a manifestation of a misogyny that has been with us much longer than the church has. Yet it would never have occurred to my husband and me not to be married in a Catholic church, not to have our children baptized.

On hospital forms and in political polls, while others leave the space blank or say "none of your business," I have no hesitation about giving my religion.

We are cultural Catholics. I once sneered at that expression, used by Jewish friends at college, only because I was not introspective enough to understand how well it applied to me. Catholicism is to us now not so much a system of beliefs or a set of laws but a shared history. It is not so much our faith as our past. The tenets of the church which I learned as a child have ever since been at war with the facts of my adult life. The Virgin Birth. The Trinity. The Resurrection. Why did God make me? God made me to know Him, to love Him, and to serve Him in this world and to be happy with Him forever in the next. I could recite parts of the Baltimore Catechism in my sleep. Do I believe those words? I don't know. What I do believe are those guidelines that do not vary from faith to faith, that are as true of Judaism or Methodism as they are of Catholicism: that people should be kind to one another, that they should help those in need, that they should respect others as they wish to be respected.

And I believe in my own past. I was educated by nuns, given absolution by priests. My parents were married in a Catholic church, my grandparents and mother buried from one. Saturday afternoons kneeling on Leatherette pads in the dim light of the confessional, listening for the sound of the priest sliding back the grille on his side. Sunday mornings kneeling with my face in my hands, the Communion wafer stuck to the roof of my dry mouth. These are my history. I could no more say I am not Catholic than say I am not Irish, not Italian. Yet I have never been to Ireland or Italy.

Some of our Jewish friends have returned to the ways of their past, to Shabbat without automobiles and elevators, to dietary laws and the study of Hebrew. We cannot do the same. There is no longer a Latin Mass, no Communion fast from midnight on. Even the inn is gone from the Bible; now Mary and Joseph are turned away from "the place where travelers lodged."

The first time my husband and I went to midnight mass on Christmas Eve in our parish church, we arrived a half-hour early so we would get a seat. When the bells sounded twelve and the priest came down the center aisle, his small acolytes in their child-size cassocks walking before him, the pews were still half empty. We were thinking of a different time, when the churches were packed, when missing Mass was a sin, when we still believed that that sort of sin existed—sins against rules, victimless sins.

There are more families coming to that church now, families like us with very small children who often have to leave before the Gospel because of tears, fatigue, temper tantrums. (I remember that, when I was growing up, my family's parish church was shaped like a cross, and one of the short arms was for the women with babies. It had a sheet of glass walling it off and was soundproof. And through the glass you could see the babies, as though in a movie with no audio, their little mouths round, their faces red. Inside that room, the noise was dreadful. But missing Mass was a sin.)

I think perhaps those families are people like us, people who believe in something, although they are not sure what, people who feel that in a world of precious little history or tradition, this is theirs. We will pass down the story to our children: There was a woman named Mary who was visited by an angel. And the angel said, "Do not be afraid" and told her that though she was a virgin she would have a child. And He was named Jesus and was the Son of God and He rose from the dead. Everything else our children learn in America in the late twentieth century will make this sound like a fairy tale, like tales of the potato famines in Ireland and the little ramshackle houses with grape arbors on hillsides in Italy. But these are my fairy tales, and so, whether or not they are fact, they are true.

I was born a Catholic and I think I will die one. I will ask for a priest to give me Extreme Unction, as it was given to my mother, and to her mother before her. At the end, as in the beginning, I will ask for the assistance of the church, which is some fundamental part of my identity. I am a Catholic.

NUNS

The most compelling question of my girlhood was whether nuns had hair. Occasionally, when we were taken by Mother Thérèse to the yard beside the school, as we eddied about her long black legless skirts in our duffle coats and saddle shoes, a strong wind would lift the heavy black serge of her veil, and one of us—that day's celebrity—would glimpse a strand or two at the nape of her neck. For days we would conjecture whether it was merely the popular pixie cut under there, or whether her entire scalp had been shaved and what we had seen was just an oversight. A few girls of a Jesuitical turn of mind suggested that perhaps she had hair just like ours and that it was braided or pinned up. No one ever took them very seriously.

The nuns were, with the exception of my family and one or two fast friends, the most important force in my formative years. It is popular now to think of them as a joke or an anachronism, to suggest that the nuns taught little more than that a well-placed ruler hurt like the dickens and that boys were only after one thing, but that was not what I learned from them at all. I learned that women were smart and capable, could live in community together without men, and in fact did not need men much.

I am sure that being under the constant sway of human beings living in a state of enforced employment and chastity must have had some blacker reverberations, and I know the nuns attached too much value to our being well behaved, to sitting with backs straight and hands folded. But today it is the good things I remember. I suspect, deep down, that some of those women turned me into a feminist. I wonder what they would think of that? For the nuns were intelligent, most of them, and they seemed in charge. The place where they lived smelled of furniture polish and horsehair-stuffed brocade and reeked of order, and if in the morning there was chalk on their simple yet majestic habits, by afternoon it was gone.

I attended Catholic school just as the sovereignty of the church over the lives of its citizens was beginning, very slowly, to crumble. It was still a time when the Roman Catholic son who chose the priesthood beat the one who went to medical school hands down, when a Catholic daughter chose habitual pregnancy or the convent. Often it was the brightest and the most ambitious who took the latter course, which offered, in some orders, the opportunity for education and advancement. But it must have also seemed an attractive life when faced with the alternatives. I know that what I found most seductive about the convent was the place itself. Growing up in and among families where children—in various stages of undress, distress, and toilet training—outnumbered adults, I thought it was a place of wonderful peace and quiet. There were no fingerprints on the mahogany table tops.

My recollection is that the woman who founded the order that taught me, a somewhat upper-crusty group that ran private rather than mere parochial schools, had even been a wife and mother and had thrown it over for the convent. The story was that her husband decided he had a calling for the priesthood and somehow got a dispensation to follow it despite a sizable family, and his wife then decided to enter religious life. He changed his mind—that's men for you—but she refused to change hers. When I was a schoolgirl, the founder was being pushed very heavily for sainthood. No mixed messages in that story. The religious life was a higher way.

Nuns seemed sure of themselves. Perhaps, in order to style oneself a bride of Christ, self-confidence must be part of the costume. It was not their supremacy but their vulnerability that we found most disturbing. On those rare occasions when Mother Thérèse wept, it seemed to me that a certain surety in life disappeared. It occurs to me now, of course, that she was high-strung, quite young, and very pretty, and that seventh grade combined with poverty, chastity, and obedience must have been heavy going. And we often gave her good reason to cry.

I never heard a word about sex from the nuns. I learned that clunker about patent-leather shoes reflecting up from a fat girl who had older sisters when both of us were in fifth grade. There were only two kinds of men I ever saw the sisters with: the priests, upon whom they danced attendance with an air both deferential and slightly flirtatious, and our fathers, who were either hangdog and very proper, or embarrassingly jovial and jokey. I know now that the sisters were in masculine thrall, both to Rome and to various philanthropists, relying on one for the rules by which they lived and the other for the money and the clothes and the house in which to do the living. But it seemed to me that they took good care of themselves.

I always thought the nuns were somehow sterner and less warm with the boys than with the girls, although my husband says he had a teacher who thought the girls were second-rate because they could never become priests. And there was always one—I remember mine as vividly as if she were glaring over the top of this page, hissing, "Miss Quindlen, is that you whispering in the back of my classroom?"—who was mean and angry and sadistic. But most of them were like Sister Mary Luke, tall, pale, her enfolding embrace exaggerated by her uniform capelet, who was wonderful with playground spills and played a mean game of volleyball; or Mother Mary Ephrem, who made me learn a new, arcane word from the dictionary every day of eighth grade so that someday I would be doing precisely what I am doing now.

I remember the sisters running down a hockey field or out on the polished wood of the basketball court, driving or dribbling, their voluminous skirts held up by huge safety pins that they always kept pinned to their bodices. I was amazed to hear from other girls that *athletics* were only for boys; a Catholic schoolgirl learns *sports*, led by a nun.

Above all it seemed to me that the nuns who taught us had their own lives—much more so than my mother, who was parceled out to many others, our family's community property. I always pictured the sisters, each with a cool white bedroom in the top reaches of their stone house, no rug on the floor, a crucifix over the bed, books on the bureau. One of my most enduring memories is the last day of school each year, when we would fly down the street and they would stand on the steps and wave, waiting until the last child was gone before turning back and readying the classrooms for their long rest. I never saw the nuns during the summer months. I always wondered if they went swimming, and, if so, what they wore. I imagined this community of capable women gathered at a beach house somewhere, in white habits instead of their workaday black, playing volleyball, batting the ball back and forth over the net, their ankles flashing.

KEEPING
THE
FAITH

The first year I was in Catholic school there were, on the long wall of the convent parlor, portraits of two men in rococo gilt frames. One was an imagined rendering of Jesus Christ, wearing a gold robe. The other was a color photograph of a rather dour man in much more elaborate garments, wearing the sort of austere rimless glasses that would later be affected by rock-and-roll musicians and college students. This was Pope Pius XII, who from his likeness appeared to be stern and unapproachable. We knew that he was the closest thing we had to God on earth at the time.

John Paul II seems to me, in face and in fact, to be a man warmer and more human than that predecessor of his, four popes ago. But that is not why I think of him as a man rather than a near-deity. I have changed since the afternoons I spent in the convent parlor, and so has the faith in which I was raised. I find my religion within my heart, not within the hierarchy of the Roman Catholic church.

When the Pope was here in 1979 and I covered the occasion, I found myself unaccountably moved by his visit despite the fact that I felt his influence in my life was negligible. It is the same way I felt the last time I saw the White House: deeply aware of a long and venerable history of which I am one tiny part, despite the fact that the person who leads the historical tradition at this moment is someone whose deepest beliefs are at odds with my own.

We have had an odd history, the people of my generation. When we were children, sexual mores were one way, and now they are another. National feeling was one way, and now it is another. Sexual politics were one way, and now they are another.

For those of us who grew up Catholic, the change has been similar. When we were young, the convents and seminaries were full. Now it is difficult to find young men and women with religious vocations. The Mass was said in Latin. Now, of course, in this country it is in English. Our lives were filled with a host of rules, regulations, and religious formulas. Most of them are gone. So are many of the parishioners. On Easter in our parish church the priest walked to the altar, looked out over the aisles crammed with people of all ages, and said wryly, "You know, we have this Mass every Sunday." At Communion, the little children, those too young to receive the sacrament, were called up to the altar rail for the first time in their lives, to be given a cookie in the shape of the Paschal lamb. There was the tragedy: What if they finally had a church that knew how to care for its people, and nobody came?

Many of my friends have fled a Catholicism that, for some of us, no longer exists. It happens to be a Catholicism they see embodied in this Pope and his pronouncements on such matters as birth control, the ordination of women, and homosexuality. It is a Catholicism of "Thou shalt not." I know it still exists much below the hierarchy. The last time I wrote a column about being a Catholic, I got lots of hard, mean, judgmental letters from people who said "Oh no, you're not," people anxious to exclude rather than include, people who seemed ignorant of the commandment I was taught was the greatest of all. Love one another.

For Catholics of my age, the central event of our maturation was the collection of changes and modifications now generally known as Vatican II. The central figure was John XXIII, who was to our religion what John Kennedy was to our government. That Pope changed our lives, and not just because the rites of the church were now in the language of the schoolyard. It was because what John XXIII seemed to be saying was that the spirit of the law was more important than the letter. That to be kind and considerate was more important than keeping your mantilla on. That to do good was as important as to do penance. It was the Catholicism of "Father, forgive them." That is the faith in which I have remained. It is one in which the messages of your heart and your conscience take precedence over messages from Rome. Those who still shun the judgmental and authoritarian Catholicism that they are convinced triumphed over the changes of Vatican II are skeptical, particularly now, with a charismatic and deeply intellectual Pope who condemns *in vitro* fertilization and welcomes Kurt Waldheim. But in a quiet, steady, almost sub rosa way others are following their hearts. Several recent polls show that the vast majority of Catholics believe they can be true to their faith while disagreeing with its earthly leader.

I have thought several times this week of an incident that took place ten years ago. My fiancé and I went to Cana conferences, the sessions that prepare young Catholics for marriage within the church. They were conducted by a priest we both knew well and loved. I was nervous, because we were living together, using birth control, but especially because I was not sure that I ever wanted to have children, and knew that he would be bound to ask about that. When he did, I could tell by his face that he had seen something click shut in mine. "Wait a minute," he said. "Let me put it this way. Have you totally ruled out having children?" Both of us immediately leapt in: Oh, no, Father, no; absolutely not.

He knew my doubt about doing something which is absolutely essential to the spirit of Catholic matrimony. But he knew, too, a little something about the human spirit, and about trying to look beyond people's words into their hearts. He would have been perfectly justified in asking that question exactly the way it was meant to be asked, and, given the equivocal answer I was likely to give, to refuse to marry us. He could have considered us unfit according to the letter of the law. But according to its spirit he knew we were good people, who would try to be good to others. He knew it, too, on the days he baptized our two children.

TAKING
A
STAND

FEMINIST

would like to say that I became a feminist to make the world better for women everywhere, but in truth it was to make the world better for me. This was almost twenty years ago, and altruism was not my strong suit; to paraphrase Rhett Butler, the only cause I believed in was me. Nor was I struck by the rank injustice of sex discrimination. It just seemed like men got all the good stuff.

I grew up in a city run by men, in a church run by men, in a household run by a man. Men had comfortable shoes, a life outside the home, and money in their wallets. Women had children, who are wonderful but not sufficient unto themselves, at least for me. The best job you could get as a woman then involved a lifetime vow of chastity, which was not my thing. I figured either life was going to be considerably different for me than it was for my mother, or I was going to be angry all the time. I jumped on the bandwagon. I've never gotten off.

As I watched the convention of the National Organization for Women on television the other night, I realized my only real political identification has been with womens' rights. It is the only cause I have ever believed in that has improved the world. Life for many women is not the same as it was when I was young, and I do not believe it will ever be so again. I do not believe that ever again will there be a handful of token women in the graduating class at Harvard Law School. I do not believe that ever again will there be a handful of female New York City police officers.

Change is exceedingly slow, but somehow sure. My friend the female rabbi still meets up with the occasional father of the bride who will not pay for the wedding if she officiates. To write that sentence alone is a measure of the shock of the new, and the stubborn strength of the old. On the one hand, the father of the bride and his wallet. On the other, a rabbi who is a woman.

I went to a women's college. Not long ago I was asked what it was like. At the time I was speaking at a college that until 1969 had been all-male and fiercely proud to be so. I said it was a little like learning to swim while holding on to the side of the pool; I didn't learn the arm movements until after I graduated, but by that time I was one hell of a kicker.

When I began school there were still marks on the university buildings made by student demonstrators. Perhaps that was why some of us were happy to view our own feminism as a liberal and not a radical political movement. A liberal movement is precisely what we got. We were permitted limited access to the world of men provided that to some considerable extent we mimicked their behavior but did not totally alter our own.

I suppose we sometimes feel disappointed with our circumstances today because now that the liberal movement has taken place, now that women are performing cardiac surgery and becoming members of the welders' unions, it has become clearer than ever that what we really needed was a radical movement. We have given the word an ominous connotation, but in fact it means only a root change. We needed a root change in the way things work: in the way everyone approached work, in the way everyone approached the care of children, in the way everyone, male and female, approached the balance of life and work and obligations and inclinations. I do not think this really came about.

Everyone now accepts that men, too, can cry, but women still often have more reason to. "We must fight for parental leaves for mothers and fathers," one feminist told me, and I knew she was right, except that I didn't know many men who were going to take paternity leaves if they were offered. I suppose we must fight to raise sons who will take them.

We still find ourselves dependent on the kindness of strangers, from Supreme Court justices to husbands and lovers. I do not believe that we are likely to go back to a time when patients refuse to be treated by female doctors, but I think we could go back to a time when doctors of both sexes are forbidden by law to perform abortions. I think that institutions run by men, with a sprinkling of women in high places, may begin to feel self-congratulatory and less enthusiastic about hiring and promotion efforts about which they have always been ambivalent.

It is difficult to communicate some of the terror of this to young women who have grown up with a sense of entitlement, who were born in the year in which a bin was filled with undergarments on the Atlantic City boardwalk in protest of the Miss America pageant, who grew up knowing that they could go to Princeton or rabbinical school or the moon if they worked at it hard enough, who have never been asked how fast they typed.

Some have told me that they do not think of themselves as feminists, that they are a generation of individualists who do not align themselves with a group cause, particularly one which represents battles they believe have been largely won.

Perhaps it was a particularly female thing about me, but I did not feel qualified, when I was young, to be an individualist. I felt that by birth I was part of a group, and that the signal hallmark of that group was that they were denied access to money and power by virtue of biology. That seemed over-whelming to me at seventeen, and it seemed to present me with two choices. One was to distinguish myself from other women. The other was to stand up for the rights of women as a group. I wasn't capable of going it alone. Luckily, I didn't have to. I had my sisters.

DIRTY
BOOK

remember with great clarity the afternoon my
mother, an exceedingly gentle soul, hurled the
current best seller across the living room with
such force that it bounced off the wall opposite.
"It's a dirty book," she said, nostrils flaring, as she
saw my face, and she stomped off into the
kitchen. It was some measure of how rattled she
was that she left the book itself, its yellow jacket
a bright blot on the carpet, in the same room
with a teenager whose paperback copy of *The
Group* fell open automatically to Dottie's de-
flowering.

The book was *Portnoy's Complaint,* and I
thought it was wonderful. I understood what my
mother meant—the breaks in the binding indicated that she had pitched the book just at the
pivotal liver scene—but it seemed to me that the
sex was so central to, so much a part of the extraordinary humor and tone that to be offended
by it was beside the point. I tried to tell her this,

but she could not be persuaded. And so I came to see vividly that reasonable people could disagree about whether something was obscene.

Naturally, this came to mind when the commission headed by Attorney General Edwin Meese III released its report on pornography. But I had thought of it many times before, because, of all the areas in which generations are divided from one another, the subject of sex is the one where they are least likely to meet. My grandmother once caused a great stir on the beach at Atlantic City because she and her best friend were among the first to venture forth on the sand wearing one-piece bathing suits instead of the bloomers and skirts and overblouses that were then the norm. I, on the other hand, had to decide on my honeymoon whether to be the only person on a Caribbean island wearing the top to my bikini. It is inevitable that we two would have disparate views about the propriety and obscenity of displaying the nude human body. This is not because my grandmother is old-fashioned and I am modern—I sometimes think my grandmother is about as old-fashioned as the Concorde—but simply because of the disparate climates in which we learned about, became accustomed to, and made our personal peace with sex.

And so I was in part distressed about the Meese commission because it did not seem very much like a jury of my peers. Mostly, of course, I didn't like the idea of a jury of any sort. The commission seemed to spend a lot of time talking about sex with children, torture, and rape, which seem to me things that all reasonable people, regardless of their ages, agree are wrong. I'm under the impression that there are laws having nothing to do with pornography that make such acts illegal whenever they are performed. But reasonable people can surely disagree about some of the other material the commission examined: skin magazines, X-rated movies, the kind of material that most people my age have been exposed to over and over again.

The idea of outlawing pornography makes me remember the box spring and the mattress. I don't know when it was that parents decided that the space between the two was a good place to put their so-called dirty books—which in most cases were marriage manuals and the odd copy of *Tropic of Cancer*—but it was a good place for curious kids; we all knew just where to find them. In my home, the marriage manuals, or whatever you call *The Joy of Sex,* will stay on the shelf and off the box spring. After all, while my mother's mother told her nothing about sex, and my mother told me the basics when I was ten (which I gather from my friends made her something of a pioneer), on some days it seems as if I will have to tell my almost-three-year-old the facts of life in the next fifteen minutes.

Will the illustrations in *The Joy of Sex* titillate my sons when they are in their early teens? Probably. (My recollection of teenage boys is that they can get worked up over women's underwear flapping on a clothesline.) Is it pornography? Of course not. Would it have been so classified when my mother was a girl? Without a doubt.

Mores change. Fifteen years ago my father, like lots of others, said that if a daughter of his lived in sin before she was married, she'd be off his Thanksgiving dinner list. Today, he says he thinks cohabitation is sometimes a good preparation for a lifetime together. Fifteen years ago, I thought *Playboy* was pretty lewd. Now, I think the centerfolds are simply silly, and that all those women miming sexual ecstasy in bizarre undergarments succeed only in looking as if they have bad colds. And nearly fifteen years ago I saw my first pornographic movie. I was twenty-one, and a city editor with an odd sense of humor sent me to sit through *Deep Throat* with a judge who was ruling on some obscenity issue. I thought the judge was going to have a stroke when he saw, not Linda Lovelace, but me watching Linda Lovelace.

It would be some feat to come up with a standard of obscenity that reflects my experiences; those of my mother, who was as perturbed by the fleeting flash of breasts as she was by the blood in the *Psycho* shower scene, and those of my grandmother, who lived through the enormous brouhaha over the "damn" in the last scene of *Gone With the Wind*. That's why it's so terrific that, until now, we have set such standards for ourselves. Those who make movies of people beating up other people should be arrested as an accessory to assault. That's not a crime of sex, but a crime of violence. Meanwhile, I would like to maintain the obscenity standards set so well by my mother and me that afternoon in our living room. She exercised her personal right to throw a dirty book at the wall, and I exercised my personal right to read it and discover that it was not really dirty at all. It worked just fine then, and it will work just fine now.

HOMELESS

Her name was Ann, and we met in the Port Authority Bus Terminal several Januarys ago. I was doing a story on homeless people. She said I was wasting my time talking to her; she was just passing through, although she'd been passing through for more than two weeks. To prove to me that this was true, she rummaged through a tote bag and a manila envelope and finally unfolded a sheet of typing paper and brought out her photographs.

They were not pictures of family, or friends, or even a dog or cat, its eyes brown-red in the flashbulb's light. They were pictures of a house. It was like a thousand houses in a hundred towns, not suburb, not city, but somewhere in between, with aluminum siding and a chain-link fence, a narrow driveway running up to a one-car garage and a patch of backyard. The house was yellow. I looked on the back for a date or a name, but neither was there. There was no need for discussion. I knew what she was trying to tell me, for it was something I had often felt. She was not adrift, alone, anonymous, although her bags and her raincoat with the grime shadowing its creases had made me believe she was. She had a house, or at least once upon a time had had one. Inside were curtains, a couch, a stove, potholders. You are where you live. She was somebody.

I've never been very good at looking at the big picture, taking the global view, and I've always been a person with an overactive sense of place, the legacy of an Irish grandfather. So it is natural that the thing that seems most wrong with the world to me right now is that there are so many people with no homes. I'm not simply talking about shelter from the elements, or three square meals a day or a mailing address to which the welfare people can send the check—although I know that all these are important for survival. I'm talking about a home, about precisely those kinds of feelings that have wound up in cross-stitch and French knots on samplers over the years.

Home is where the heart is. There's no place like it. I love my home with a ferocity totally out of proportion to its appearance or location. I love dumb things about it: the hot-water heater, the plastic rack you drain dishes in, the roof over my head, which occasionally leaks. And yet it is precisely those dumb things that make it what it is—a place of certainty, stability, predictability, privacy, for me and for my family. It is where I live. What more can you say about a place than that? That is everything.

Yet it is something that we have been edging away from gradually during my lifetime and the lifetimes of my parents and grandparents. There was a time when where you lived often was where you worked and where you grew the food you ate and even where you were buried. When that era passed, where you lived at least was where your parents had lived and where you would live with your children when you became enfeebled. Then, suddenly, where you lived was where you lived for three years, until you could move on to something else and something else again.

And so we have come to something else again, to children who do not understand what it means to go to their rooms because they have never had a room, to men and women whose fantasy is a wall they can paint a color of their own choosing, to old people reduced to sitting on molded plastic chairs, their skin blue-white in the lights of a bus station, who pull pictures of houses out of their bags. Homes have stopped being homes. Now they are real estate.

People find it curious that those without homes would rather sleep sitting up on benches or huddled in doorways than go to shelters. Certainly some prefer to do so because they are emotionally ill, because they have been locked in before and they are damned if they will be locked in again. Others are afraid of the violence and trouble they may find there. But some seem to want something that is not available in shelters, and they will not compromise, not for a cot, or oatmeal, or a shower with special soap that kills the bugs. "One room," a woman with a baby who was sleeping on her sister's floor, once told me, "painted blue." That was the crux of it; not size or location, but pride of ownership. Painted blue.

This is a difficult problem, and some wise and compassionate people are working hard at it. But in the main I think we work around it, just as we walk around it when it is lying on the sidewalk or sitting in the bus terminal—the problem, that is. It has been customary to take people's pain and lessen our own participation in it by turning it into an issue, not a collection of human beings. We turn an adjective into a noun: the poor, not poor people; the homeless, not Ann or the man who lives in the box or the woman who sleeps on the subway grate.

Sometimes I think we would be better off if we forgot about the broad strokes and concentrated on the details. Here is a woman without a bureau. There is a man with no mirror, no wall to hang it on. They are not the homeless. They are people who have no homes. No drawer that holds the spoons. No window to look out upon the world. My God. That is everything.

CONDOMS

Like many American women, I know a good bit more than I'd like to about birth control, much of it garnered from books, magazines, telephone calls to friends, and raunchy conversations at bridal showers. I remember in high school when a classmate began taking The Pill and suddenly started to look like a balloon at the Macy's Thanksgiving Day parade. I remember when the women in my college dormitory gritted their teeth and had a plastic article that looked as if it had been made by Mattel placed inside their bodies. And I remember an absolutely uproarious all-female brunch where a friend described her first experience with a contraceptive device, which shot out of a bathroom window into the college quadrangle. She never retrieved it. I wouldn't have, either.

The only form of birth control none of us talked about much was the condom, because precious few of us had ever used or seen one, except at fraternity house water balloon fights. The most we had heard a man say on the subject of birth control of any kind was, "You took care of this, right?"

Condoms are of national interest now because they might slow the spread of AIDS, and while I think this is all to the good, something about it makes me furious. I know that the threat of death is more serious than pain, pelvic disease, or infertility, but I really wish someone had thought about a campaign for condoms fifteen years ago.

Perhaps the posters could have carried a picture of the Dalkon Shield. It's a horrible-looking thing, that I.U.D., like one of those oversize pictures of a tick, with its fat round body and splayed plastic legs. But it's even more horrible to talk to women who used it and who weep as they speak, who have had ectopic pregnancies that blew their Fallopian tubes apart or pelvic disease that left them with scar tissue. If we knew then what we know now, perhaps they'd be having children instead of surgery. If we knew then what we know now, perhaps there would have been condom commercials encouraging men to "give the women you love a break—use a condom." But when we were becoming sexually active, condoms were a joke, and the joke was on us. Most of the time, women had sole responsibility for birth control.

Now, as then, some men do not use condoms because they are "sort of a drag," as one man told me (as opposed to birth control for women, which has sometimes led to a stroke or sterility). Perhaps this is changing, since dying of AIDS is obviously much more of a drag than using a condom. But some heterosexual men and women still seem more interested in denial than protection, much less male contraception.

Recently, I talked to the doctor who runs the health services office for a women's college. She said that many students were asking the clinic for condoms. I also talked to students, and said I was pleased that, while protecting their lives, they were also persuading men to participate in birth control. I was somehow not surprised when this statement turned out to be wrong. Some of the women had gotten condoms and then stashed them in their underwear drawer. And there they sat, right next to the little wheel of pills or the plastic diaphragm case. These women were confident enough in their relationships to sleep with their boyfriends, confident enough to assume their boyfriends did not have AIDS, but not confident enough to ask those boyfriends to do something they might not want to do. The women, too, had heard that condoms were sort of a drag.

I've never met a woman who exactly loved her method of birth control, but that doesn't seem to have inhibited women from using it. The bottom line has always been that this is because we are the ones who get pregnant, which is true. But pregnancy and birth and all they entail have changed in the past fifteen years. We have seen men go to court to halt abortions and adoptions, insisting that fathers are just as important as mothers. We have seen the presence of fathers in the delivery room change from a curiosity to a commonplace. When the pregnancy test is positive, we even say that "we are pregnant."

But while society has come to expect participatory fathers, it does not expect participatory birth control. Women who take the pill don't blow up like a balloon the way they once did, nor can women purchase an I.U.D. in the United States, because of the sheer number of lawsuits brought against their manufacturers. But one thing hasn't changed: women still take care of birth control.

Women take care of business. That's why condom manufacturers are marketing directly to us now, even though most of the American men who have contracted AIDS don't even sleep with women. We took care of business when we were trying to inhibit conception. I suppose everyone assumes that we'll take care of business when it's time to inhibit death, too.

I suppose everyone is right. It still makes me angry. The manufacturer's insert in a package of birth-control pills says you should take them under a doctor's supervision: "They can be associated with serious side effects, which may be fatal," the insert says, including blood clots in the lungs and brain, liver tumors, high blood pressure, gall-bladder disease. None of those are associated with condom use.

SOME THOUGHTS ABOUT ABORTION

t was always the look on their faces that told me first. I was the freshman dormitory counselor and they were the freshmen at a women's college where everyone was smart. One of them would come into my room, a golden girl, a valedictorian, an 800 verbal score on the S.A.T.'s, and her eyes would be empty, seeing only a busted future, the devastation of her life as she knew it. She had failed biology, messed up the math; she was pregnant.

That was when I became pro-choice.

It was the look in his eyes that I will always remember, too. They were as black as the bottom of a well, and in them for a few minutes I thought I saw myself the way I had always wished to be—clear, simple, elemental, at peace. My child looked at me and I looked back at him in the delivery room, and I realized that out of a sea of infinite possibilities it had come down to this: a specific person, born on the hottest day of the year, conceived on a Christmas Eve, made by his father and me miraculously from scratch.

Once I believed that there was a little blob of formless protoplasm in there and a gynecologist went after it with a surgical instrument, and that was that. Then I got pregnant myself—eagerly, intentionally, by the right man, at the right time—and I began to doubt. My abdomen still flat, my stomach roiling with morning sickness, I felt not that I had protoplasm inside, but, instead, a complete human being in miniature to whom I could talk, sing, make promises. Neither of these views was accurate; instead, I think, the reality is something in the middle. And that is where I find myself now, in the middle—hating the idea of abortions, hating the idea of having them outlawed.

For I know it is the right thing in some times and places. I remember sitting in a shabby clinic far uptown with one of those freshmen, only three months after the Supreme Court had made what we were doing possible, and watching with wonder as the lovely first love she had had with a nice boy unraveled over the space of an hour as they waited for her to be called, degenerated into sniping and silences. I remember a year or two later seeing them pass on campus and not even acknowledge each other because their conjoining had caused them so much pain, and I shuddered to think of them married, with a small psyche in their unready and unwilling hands.

I've met fourteen-year-olds who were pregnant and said they could not have abortions because of their religion, and I see in their eyes the shadows of twenty-two-year-olds I've talked to who lost their kids to foster care because they hit them or used drugs or simply had no money for food and shelter. I read not long ago about a teenager who said she meant to have an abortion but she spent the money on clothes instead: now she has a baby who turns out to be a lot more trouble than a toy. The people who hand out those execrable little pictures of dismembered fetuses at abortion clinics seem to forget the extraordinary pain children may endure after they are born when they are unwanted, even hated, or simply tolerated.

I believe that in a contest between the living and the almost living, the latter must, if necessary, give way to the will of the former. That is what the fetus is to me, the almost living. These questions began to plague me—and, I've discovered, a good many other women—after I became pregnant. But they became even more acute after I had my second child, mainly because he is so different from his brother. On two random nights eighteen months apart the same two people managed to conceive, and on one occasion the tumult within turned itself into a curly-haired brunet with merry black eyes who walked and talked late and loved the whole world, and on another it became a blond with hazel Asian eyes and a pug nose who tried to conquer the world almost as soon as he entered it.

If we were to have an abortion next time for some reason or another, which infinite possibility becomes, not a reality, but a nullity? The girl with the blue eyes? The improbable redhead? The natural athlete? The thinker? My husband, ever at the heart of the matter, put it another way. Knowing he is finding two children somewhat more overwhelming than he expected, I asked if he would want me to have an abortion if I accidentally became pregnant again right away. "And waste a perfectly good human being?" he said.

Coming to this quandary has been difficult for me. In fact, I believe the issue of abortion is difficult for all thoughtful people. I don't know anyone who has had an abortion who has been casual about it. If there is one thing I find intolerable about most of the so-called right-to-lifers, it is that they try to portray abortion rights as something that feminists thought up on a slow Saturday over a light lunch. That is nonsense. I also know that some people who support abortion rights are most comfortable with a monolithic position because it seems the strongest front against the smug and sometimes violent opposition.

But I don't feel all one way about abortion anymore, and I don't think it serves a just cause to pretend that many of us do. For years I believed that a woman's right to choose was absolute, but now I wonder. Do I, with a stable home and marriage and sufficient stamina and money, have the freedom to choose abortion because a pregnancy is inconvenient just now? Legally I do have the right; legally I want always to have that right. It is the morality of exercising it under those circumstances that makes me wonder.

Technology has foiled us. The second trimester has become a time of resurrection; a fetus at six months can be one woman's late abortion, another's premature, viable child. Photographers now have film of embryos the size of a grape, oddly human, flexing their fingers, sucking their thumbs. Women have amniocentisis to find out whether they are carrying a child with birth defects that they may choose to abort. Before the procedure, they must have a sonogram, one of those fuzzy black-and-white photos like a love song heard through static on the radio, which shows someone is in there.

I have taped on my VCR a public television program in which somehow, inexplicably, a film is shown of a fetus *in utero* scratching its face, seemingly putting up a tiny hand to shield itself from the camera's eye. It would make a potent weapon in the arsenal of the antiabortionists. I grow sentimental about it as it floats in the salt water, part fish, part human being. It is almost living, but not quite. It has almost turned my heart around, but not quite turned my head.

GETTING INVOLVED

t was a summer night when I heard the running footsteps behind me. I ran, too, and slipped into the hallway of my building, a locked door, a pane of glass insulating me from the outside. The woman was only a few steps behind me. Her face on the other side of the glass was black with mascara mixed with tears. She said someone had tried to rape her, and that she thought he was following close behind.

It occurred to me afterward that everyone should be allowed more than a minute to suddenly discover what sort of person they are. That was all it took for me to play out the possibilities: a gang of thieves who used a seemingly distraught woman as their entrée, an unbalanced street person who would turn on me in the safe confinement of my own home. Or a rape victim.

I opened the door.

She had a cup of tea, refused to call the police, washed her face, apologized, and finally, after an

hour, went home in a cab. I was left with the teacup, the
blackened tissues, and an unbearable sense that the rapist had
watched her enter and was now lying in wait for me. Each time
I thought of the woman, I had a heavy, deep feeling in my
chest that I finally recognized as rage—not at her pursuer, but
at her.

I hadn't thought of that night in some ten years until lately,
when I have wondered again about the responsibilities of one
human being toward others of the species. There are two
women that have made me consider this: Cheryl Pierson and
Hedda Nussbaum. Both of their cases have made me think of
another, too—that of Kitty Genovese.

Miss Pierson went to jail, after she paid a high school classmate to kill her father because, she said, her father would not
keep his hands off her, because he sometimes had sexual inter-
course with her two and three times a day. Miss Nussbaum
went to jail, too, accused with her lover of beating their six-
year-old adopted daughter to death. In photographs taken at
the time of her arraignment, she looks stunned, but perhaps
that is simply a function of her face, the face of an aging
prizefighter who has gone back for the TKO many times too
many. Clearly, it was not only the little girl who was beaten.

Two horrible secrets. But, of course, people knew. They
always do. When Miss Pierson first alleged that her father had
molested her, she said that she had been afraid to tell anyone.
And then one friend, neighbor, relative after another appeared
in court to say that they suspected, that they had watched the
man grab his daughter's body, make dirty comments about it.
But nothing was really done until a boy Cheryl Pierson sat next
to in homeroom shot Mr. Pierson in the driveway of the Pierson house.

The horror show in Miss Nussbaum's apartment was an
open secret, too. Neighbors heard screams and shouts and the
unmistakable sound of something hitting a human being, hard,

even through the thick walls of an old building. Some of them saw bruises on the little girl. The difference between this and the Pierson case was that some of them did something. Some of them sought help from police and social service agencies for the people on the other side of the wall. But nothing really was done until the morning when Hedda Nussbaum and Joel Steinberg were taken into custody, their adopted son taken to a foster home, and their little girl taken to the hospital, where she was pronounced brain dead.

And so to Kitty Genovese, twenty-three years dead. She was a national symbol. She was knifed to death and her neighbors listened and watched and, the modern parable went, did nothing. At the time there were two reactions to the story: that it could not have happened, and that, if it did, it could only have happened in New York City.

But it doesn't only happen in New York, and it happens all the time. We have a national character that helps it along. The rugged individualists who take care of themselves, the independent men and women who prize the freedom to manage their lives without outside interference: these are the essential Americans. We want a police force that respects the rights of individuals, the same police force that will not take a man into custody, even if his wife's face looks like chopped meat, if she insists she fell in the bathroom.

But the dark side to independence is isolation, and the dark side to managing your own life a belief that it must be perfectly managed. "Dirty laundry," we call our problems, and "Don't trouble trouble," we say. There are countries in which the answer to "How are you?" is often "Not so good." Here the answer is almost always "Fine." There are cultures in which family members get together and tell you what you are doing wrong and how to live your life. I prefer one in which everyone minds their own business—at least until that moment when I am yelling "Help!"

So sometimes the victims feel that it is impossible or unseemly to pass their problems on to another, that in the midst of self-reliance they would be blamed for having pain, or sharing it. Sometimes the bystanders feel that if there was real trouble, the victims would do something about it, that the Cheryl Piersons and the Hedda Nussbaums would call hot lines and find therapists, that when the authorities have been notified there is not much more they can be expected to do. In retrospect, of course, it is never enough. The storm breaks, the man is murdered, the child beaten to death, and people realize that, in some sense, they have been watching it all through their curtains. Life as spectator sport.

That's why I was so angry that night, when one of the players demanded with her streaked cheeks and her sobs that I come down out of the bleachers and help her out. I was taking care of my own life and I had no interest in being implicated in anyone else's. How dare a stranger pass on her vulnerability. There was nothing I could do anyway. There was no way I could help. But at least I opened the door. If I had known then what I know now, I probably wouldn't have. I would have gone upstairs and called the police, which seems a sensible, no-risk solution. Except that when I came back down she might not have been there. Perhaps she would have been somewhere with a knife at her throat. On the other hand, I would have made the right decision—for me. And I could always say I tried.

SEX ED

everal years ago I spent the day at a family planning clinic in one of New York City's poorest
neighborhoods. I sat around a Formica table with
a half-dozen sixteen-year-old girls and listened
with some amazement as they showed off their
knowledge of human sexuality.

They knew how long sperm lived inside the
body, how many women out of a hundred using
a diaphragm were statistically likely to get pregnant and the medical term for the mouth of the
cervix. One girl pointed out all the parts of the
female reproductive system on a placard; another
recited the stages of the ovulation cycle from day
one to twenty-eight. There was just one problem
with this performance: although the results of
their laboratory tests would not be available for
fifteen more minutes, every last one of them was
pregnant.

I always think of that day when someone sug-
gests that sex education at school is a big part of

the answer to the problem of teenage pregnancy. I happen to be a proponent of such programs; I think human sexuality is a subject for dispassionate study, like civics and ethics and dozens of other topics that have a moral component. I'd like my sons to know as much as possible about how someone gets pregnant, how pregnancy can be avoided, and what it means when avoidance techniques have failed.

I remember adolescence about as vividly as I remember anything, however, and I am not in the least convinced that that information alone will significantly alter the rate of teenage pregnancy. It seemed to me that day in the clinic, and on days I spent at schools and on street corners, that teenage pregnancy has a lot more to do with what it means to be a teenager than with how someone gets pregnant. When I was in high school, at the tail end of the sixties, there was a straightforward line on sex among my friends. Boys could have it; girls couldn't. A girl who was not a virgin pretended she was. A girl who was sleeping with her boyfriend, no matter how longplaying the relationship, pretended she was not.

It is the nature of adolescence that there is no past and no future, only the present, burning as fierce, bright, and merciless as a bare light bulb. Girls had sex with boys because nothing seemed to matter except right now, not pregnancy, not parental disapprobation, nothing but those minutes, this dance, that face, those words. Most of them knew that pregnancy could result, but they assured themselves that they would be the lucky ones who would not get caught. Naturally, some of them were wrong, and in my experience they did one of three things: they went to Puerto Rico for a mysterious weekend trip; visited an aunt in some faraway state for three months and came back with empty eyes and a vague reputation, or got married, quickly, in Empire-waist dresses.

What seems to have changed most since then is that there is little philosophical counterpoint, hypocritical or not, to the raging hormones of adolescence, and that so many of the once-hidden pregnancies are hidden no more.

Not long after the day at the family planning clinic, I went to a public high school in the suburbs. In the girl's room was this graffito: Jennifer Is a Virgin. I asked the kids about it and they said it was shorthand for geek, nerd, weirdo, somebody who was so incredibly out of it that they were in high school and still hadn't had sex. If you were a virgin, they told me, you just lied about it so that no one would think you were that immature. The girls in the family planning clinic told me much the same thing—that everyone did it, that the boys wanted it, that not doing it made them seem out of it. The only difference, really, was that the girls in the clinic were poor and would have their babies, and the girls in the high school were well-to-do and would have abortions. Pleasure didn't seem to have very much to do with sex for either group. After she learned she was pregnant, one of the girls at the clinic said, without a trace of irony, that she hoped childbirth didn't hurt as much as sex had. Birth control was easily disposed of in both cases. The pill, the youngsters said, could give you a stroke; the IUD could make you sterile. A diaphragm was disgusting.

One girl told me the funniest thing her boyfriend—a real original thinker—had told her: they couldn't use condoms because it was like taking a shower with a raincoat on. She was a smart girl, and pretty, and I wanted to tell her that it sounded as if she was sleeping with a jerk who didn't deserve her. But that is the kind of basic fact of life that must be taught not in the classroom, not by a stranger, but at home by the family. It is this that, finally, I will try to teach my sons about sex, after I've explained fertile periods and birth control and all the other mechanics that are important to understand but never really go to the heart of the matter: I believe I will say that when you sleep with someone you take off a lot more than your clothes.

EXECUTION

Ted Bundy and I go back a long way, to a time
when there was a series of unsolved murders in
Washington State known only as the Ted murders. Like a lot of reporters, I'm something of a
crime buff. But the Washington Ted murders—
and the ones that followed in Utah, Colorado,
and finally in Florida, where Ted Bundy was convicted and sentenced to die—fascinated me because I could see myself as one of the victims. I
looked at the studio photographs of young
women with long hair, pierced ears, easy smiles,
and I read the descriptions: polite, friendly, quick
to help, eager to please. I thought about being
approached by a handsome young man asking for
help, and I knew if I had been in the wrong place
at the wrong time I would have been a goner. By
the time Ted finished up in Florida, law enforce-
ment authorities suspected he had murdered dozens of young women. He and the death penalty
seemed made for each other.

The death penalty and I, on the other hand, seem to have nothing in common. But Ted Bundy has made me think about it all over again, now that the outlines of my sixties liberalism have been filled in with a decade as a reporter covering some of the worst back alleys in New York City and three years as a mother who, like most, would lay down her life for her kids. Simply put, I am opposed to the death penalty. I would tell that to any judge or lawyer undertaking the voir dire of jury candidates in a state in which the death penalty can be imposed. That is why I would be excused from such a jury. In a rational, completely cerebral way, I think the killing of one human being as punishment for the killing of another makes no sense and is inherently immoral.

But whenever my response to an important subject is rational and completely cerebral, I know there is something wrong with it —and so it is here. I have always been governed by my gut, and my gut says I am hypocritical about the death penalty. That is, I do not in theory think that Ted Bundy, or others like him, should be put to death. But if my daughter had been the one clubbed to death as she slept in a Tallahassee sorority house, and if the bite mark left in her buttocks had been one of the prime pieces of evidence against the young man charged with her murder, I would with the greatest pleasure kill him myself.

The State of Florida will not permit the parents of Bundy's victims to do that, and, in a way, that is the problem with an emotional response to capital punishment. The only reason for a death penalty is to exact retribution. Is there anyone who really thinks that it is a deterrent, that there are considerable numbers of criminals out there who think twice about committing crimes because of the sentence involved? The ones I have met in my professional duties have either sneered at the justice system, where they can exchange one charge for another with more ease than they could return a shirt to a clothing store, or they have simply believed that it is the other guy who will get caught, get convicted, get the stiffest sentence. Of course, the death penalty would act as a deterrent by eliminating recidivism, but then so would life without parole, albeit at greater taxpayer expense.

I don't believe deterrence is what most proponents seek from the death penalty anyhow. Our most profound emotional response is to want criminals to suffer as their victims did. When a man is accused of throwing a child from a high-rise terrace, my emotional—some might say hysterical—response is that he should be given an opportunity to see how endless the seconds are from the thirty-first story to the ground. In a civilized society that will never happen. And so what many people want from the death penalty, they will never get.

Death is death, you may say, and you would be right. But anyone who has seen someone die suddenly of a heart attack and someone else slip slowly into the clutches of cancer knows that there are gradations of dying.

I watched a television reenactment one night of an execution by lethal injection. It was well done; it was horrible. The methodical approach, people standing around the gurney waiting, made it more awful. One moment there was a man in a prone position; the next moment that man was gone. On another night I watched a television movie about a little boy named Adam Walsh, who disappeared from a shopping center in Florida. There was a reenactment of Adam's parents coming to New York, where they appeared on morning talk shows begging for their son's return, and in their hotel room, where they received a call from the police saying that Adam had just been found: not all of Adam, actually, just his severed head, discovered in the waters of a Florida canal. There is nothing anyone could do that is bad enough for an adult who took a six-year-old boy away from his parents, perhaps tortured, then murdered him and cut off his head. Nothing at all. Lethal injection? The electric chair? Bah.

And so I come back to the position that the death penalty is wrong, not only because it consists of stooping to the level of the killers, but also because it is not what it seems. Just before one of Ted Bundy's execution dates was postponed pending further appeals, the father of his last known victim, a twelve-year-old girl, said what almost every father in his situation must feel. "I wish they'd bring him back to Lake City," said Tom Leach of the town where Kimberly Leach lived and died, "and let us all have at him." But the death penalty does not let us all have at him in the way Mr. Leach seems to mean. What he wants is for something as horrifying as what happened to his child to happen to Ted Bundy. And that is impossible.

MAKING
NEWS

For most of my adult life, I have been an emotional hit-and-run driver—that is, a reporter. I made people like me, trust me, open their hearts and their minds to me, and cry and bleed onto the pages of my neat little notebooks, and then I went back to a safe place and made a story out of it. I am good at what I do, so often the people who read those stories cried, too. When they were done, they turned the page; when I was done, I went on to another person, another story—went from the cop's wife whose husband had never come home to the impoverished eighty-year-old Holocaust survivor to the family with the missing child. I stepped in and out of their lives as easily as I did into a pair of shoes in the morning, and when I was done I wrote my piece and went home, to the husband who had not been killed, the bank account that was full, the child safe in his high chair. Sometimes I carried within me, for a day or a week or perhaps even longer, the resonances of their pain. But they were left with the pain itself.

It was not always as bad as I've made it sound. On occasion I covered people who wanted to be covered and wrote about things that were not arrows to the heart: pothole programs, town meetings, the cost of living, the GNP. But I was good at something called human interest reporting, just at the time that human interest reporting became the vogue, and so I have spent a good deal of time in the homes of vulnerable strangers, setting up a short-term relationship, making them one-shot friends.

While they were lowering their defenses, I was maintaining my objectivity, which made it possible for me, in a kind of shorthand reminiscent of the "if u cn rd ths" ads on the subway, to put down in my notebook observations like "strokes baby's head and starts to cry" or "removes pictures of parents from drawer and tells how they were killed by SS."

I am proud of what I do, and I am ashamed of it, too. I am reasonably sensitive and not too ruthless, and so I have sometimes saved people from their own revelations and sometimes helped them by giving them the feeling that they were talking to someone who thought they were unique. I have never really understood why they talked to me. I am in one of the few businesses in which a service is provided, not to the people we deal with directly, but only to the faceless thousands who read about them. Sometimes reporters call our house to talk to my husband, who has tried newsworthy cases, and I do not miss the irony of the fact that I find them more or less a nuisance, depending on whether they call in the middle of dinner and how officious they are about the absolute necessity of their task.

Some people I have interviewed told me they thought they could help others know they were not alone, and I suspect they were right, and some people said they thought publicity might help them, and they were right, too. Occasionally I would write a story about a person in a bad spot and I would get checks for them in the mail, and I'd pass them along and think, "Well, that's good." But that wasn't why I did the stories. I did them for me.

I still do, although not on a regular basis. I still write stories and some of them are pithy explorations of unspeakable pain. I did a magazine piece not long ago about breast cancer and I sat one night in a conference room listening to eight women talk about the feeling of taking off their blouses and seeing the zipper of the scar, and I sat there, my two perfectly good breasts slowly swelling with milk for the baby at home, and felt like the worst sort of voyeur, a Peeping Tom of the emotions. Afterward some of them came to me and said how glad they were that I was writing about them, so that others would understand, and I tried to take solace from that. But all I felt was disgust at myself.

I know there are good reasons to do what I do. The more we understand worlds outside our own orbit, the better off we will be. I know there are people who do not believe reporters feel any of these things, that we file our feelings with the clippings, that both are soon dried out beyond saving. That's not true. The problem is that some time ago we invented a kind of new journalism and then tried to play it with old journalism rules. We approached a rape victim with the same feelings about objectivity and distance that we had brought to a press conference, and that was not fair—not so much to the rape victim, but to ourselves.

Some years ago I did a story about Stan and Julie Patz. Their names are probably familiar; their son, Etan, age six, disappeared in 1979, and they have opened their door to reporter after reporter because anything might bring him home. I interviewed Julie several years after he had gone, and at some point during our conversation my eyes filled and tears began. I thought I felt her pain—now that I have children of my own,

I realize I hadn't a clue to what her pain was—but I was also angry at myself for being, after years of practice and journalism review articles, so unprofessional. I thought that what was the right response for a human being was the wrong response for a reporter.

Years have passed, and Julie's son is still missing. In the meantime, I have had two sons of my own. For a while I looked for Etan's face in every playground and schoolyard, but then I stopped. I am ashamed of that. I am proud of the story I wrote. I had the story, and Julie had the life. I still think of her sometimes, and of her pain. Now that I work as a reporter less, I am capable of bringing my emotions to it more.

Perhaps there are no unwritten rules that say you are not to feel these things. Perhaps I made them up out of my own insecurities and stereotypes, the way I insisted on drinking Scotch shots when I first got into the newspaper business, so that everyone would know I was serious stuff, not just a kid. Some of this is changing for the better, I think. The day the space shuttle exploded, at the end of the evening news, it looked to me as if Dan Rather was trembling on the verge of tears when he signed off. For a moment I was able to forget the cameras hovering over the faces of Christa McAuliffe's parents as they looked up to see their eldest child blown to bits, and to forget that if I were still in the newspaper business I might have been there too, scribbling, "Mother lays head on father's shoulder." It appeared that his emotions and his profession were merging, and it made me feel a little better about myself. But the part of me that still looks at every disaster as a story wondered for just a moment if his contact lenses were bothering him, or if the light was in his eyes.

FACING THE WORST

HEREDITY

n 1971, *The New England Journal of Medicine* reported the discovery of a connection between a rare form of cancer in young women and a synthetic estrogen called diethylstilbestrol. The drug, which became known familiarly as DES, had been given to pregnant women thought to be in danger of miscarrying, and the cancer was occurring in some of their daughters. It was not until two years after the reports that I found out I was one of the young women at risk. It would be natural to think that discovering I was a DES daughter radically changed my life, but it had already been so altered the year before by my mother's death from cancer that this further fillip was only one small piece in the puzzle of why I was still alive.

At the time of my mother's illness, there was not the kind of openness about cancer that there is today, and certainly not the kind of acceptance.

I knew well that there were a handful of people who did not come to visit her because they thought what she had was catching. If that had been true, of course, my father and I would have been goners. But deep inside, I, too, believed cancer was contagious—that is, you caught it from your parents.

"Interesting but not clinically confirmed," said the emotionally dense oncologist whom I asked about hereditary links. By the time I found myself repeatedly tested for the effects of my *in utero* DES exposure, I felt like one of those teenagers in a horror movie: You don't know which closet he's in, but you do know that before the night is over he's going to jump out of there and finish you off.

For a long time this made me feel different from everyone else I knew, but slowly over the years my circle has been filled by people who carry the same feelings within them. We're not the first generation of people to feel this way; we're just the first to be afflicted with such a profound dichotomy between how we tend our bodies and how they may turn on us, about our expectations of transcending our backgrounds and the seeming tenacity of their hold.

One day not long ago I had lunch with two friends and all three of us admitted we were people who believed that the disease of our mothers would be visited on the kids. "If I can make it past forty-seven," said the one whose mother had died at that age, "then I'll be home free." And when I asked the other, whose mother had died of breast cancer, whether she did breast self-examinations, she said, in all seriousness, "No more than once a day."

There are all sorts of other diseases that have this same effect, although cancer happens to be the most prevalent and the one we hear most about. A friend of mine had a mother who died of Alzheimer's disease, and every time he misplaces his car keys he is in a sweat for a week, wondering if this is the beginning of degenerative memory loss. Another friend, whose family has a history of heart disease, lay in bed one night thinking he was having a coronary when he had really strained a shoulder muscle playing tennis.

The cumulative effect is a feeling of loss of control and a heightened sense of mortality. The second can be useful. I've had a real good time for most of the last decade because I figured that I had better get going while the going was good. But I despise the sense of helplessness. I don't know what caused my mother's cancer. I gather no one really does. Was it the air, the water, a simple predisposition, a surfeit of some food or, as one doctor suggested to me with not the slightest thought that I might be scarred by the idea, too much child bearing? Choose any or all of those things. I am still in deep trouble. My husband, whose father died of lung cancer after years of cigarette smoking and a sedentary life, does not have this sense of helplessness. He is appalled by cigarette smoking and runs four miles each morning. I wish I had such talismans.

I once talked to my grandmother about these fears, and she said the primary differences between now and then were that in her youth people didn't talk about what other people died of, they didn't think too much about what went on inside themselves, and they didn't expect to live so long. There were no warnings on cigarette packages and no oral contraceptives then, no chemotherapy and no television commercials about eating fiber to beat the Grim Reaper. When her parents died, my grandmother was grieved but not incredulous, for death was the natural corollary of life and doctors could do just so much.

Doctors now can make babies in petri dishes, and the natural corollary of life is retirement in Florida. I suppose that is what is so incongruous about what we are going through. Fresh from the gym and the sauna, I stand in the supermarket checking food labels for preservatives and wonder if there is a secret inside me, a little bit of something waiting to spring into action.

MOTHERS

The two women are sitting at a corner table in the restaurant, their shopping bags wedged between their chairs and the wall: Lord & Taylor, Bloomingdale's, something from Ann Taylor for the younger one. She is wearing a bright silk shirt, some good gold jewelry; her hair is on the long side, her makeup faint. The older woman is wearing a suit, a string of pearls, a diamond solitaire, and a narrow band. They lean across the table. I imagine the conversation: Will the new blazer go with the old skirt? Is the dress really right for an afternoon wedding? How is Daddy? How is his ulcer? Won't he slow down just a little bit?

It seems that I see mothers and daughters everywhere, gliding through what I think of as the adult rituals of parent and child. My mother died when I was nineteen. For a long time, it was all you needed to know about me, a kind of vest-pocket description of my emotional complexion: "Meet you in the lobby in ten minutes—I have long brown hair, am on the short side, have on a red coat, and my mother died when I was nineteen."

That's not true anymore. When I see a mother and a daughter having lunch in a restaurant, shopping at Saks, talking together on the crosstown bus, I no longer want to murder them. I just stare a little more than is polite, hoping that I can combine my observations with a half-remembered conversation, some anecdotes, a few old dresses, a photograph or two, and re-create, like an archaeologist of the soul, a relationship that will never exist. Of course, the question is whether it would have ever existed at all. One day at lunch I told two of my closest friends that what I minded most about not having a mother was the absence of that grown-up woman-to-woman relationship that was impossible as a child or adolescent, and that my friends were having with their mothers now. They both looked at me as though my teeth had turned purple. I didn't need to ask why; I've heard so many times about the futility of such relationships, about women with business suits and briefcases reduced to whining children by their mothers' offhand comment about a man, or a dress, or a homemade dinner.

I accept the fact that mothers and daughters probably always see each other across a chasm of rivalries. But I forget all those things when one of my friends is down with the flu and her mother arrives with an overnight bag to manage her household and feed her soup.

So now, at the center of my heart there is a fantasy, and a mystery. The fantasy is small, and silly: a shopping trip, perhaps a pair of shoes, a walk, a talk, lunch in a good restaurant, which my mother assumes is the kind of place I eat at all the time. I pick up the check. We take a cab to the train. She reminds me of somebody's birthday. I invite her and my father to dinner. The mystery is whether the fantasy has within it a nugget of fact. Would I really have wanted her to take care of the wedding arrangements, or come and stay for a week after the children were born? Would we have talked on the telephone about this and that? Would she have saved my clippings in a scrapbook? Or would she have meddled in my affairs, volunteering opinions I didn't want to hear about things that were none of her business, criticizing my clothes and my children? Worse still, would we have been strangers with nothing to say to each other? Is all the good I remember about us simply wishful thinking? Is all the bad self-protection? Perhaps it is at best difficult, at worst impossible for children and parents to be adults together. But I would love to be able to know that.

Sometimes I feel like one of those people searching, searching for the mother who gave them up for adoption. I have some small questions for her and I want the answers: How did she get her children to sleep through the night? What was her first labor like? Was there olive oil in her tomato sauce? Was she happy? If she had it to do over again, would she? When we pulled her wedding dress out of the box the other day to see if my sister might wear it, we were shocked to find how tiny it was. "My God," I said, "did you starve yourself to get into this thing?" But there was no one there. And if she had been there, perhaps I would not have asked in the first place. I suspect that we would have been friends, but I don't really know. I was simply a little too young at nineteen to understand the woman inside the mother.

I occasionally pass by one of those restaurant tables and I hear the bickering about nothing: You did so, I did not, don't tell me what you did or didn't do, oh, leave me alone. And I think that my fantasies are better than any reality could be. Then again, maybe not.

MY
GRANDMOTHER

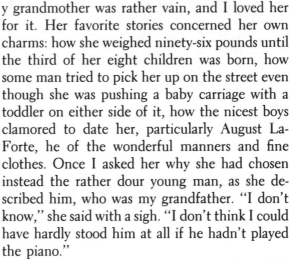

y grandmother was rather vain, and I loved her for it. Her favorite stories concerned her own charms: how she weighed ninety-six pounds until the third of her eight children was born, how some man tried to pick her up on the street even though she was pushing a baby carriage with a toddler on either side of it, how the nicest boys clamored to date her, particularly August La-Forte, he of the wonderful manners and fine clothes. Once I asked her why she had chosen instead the rather dour young man, as she described him, who was my grandfather. "I don't know," she said with a sigh. "I don't think I could have hardly stood him at all if he hadn't played the piano."

She was born Kitty O'Donnell, and she had what the nuns in school used to call a smart mouth. The older she got, the smarter it got. "How do you think your brother looks?" she asked my father several weeks ago, lying with her eyes closed in a hospital bed set up in her bedroom. "He looks fine, Mother," my father replied. "He should," she shot back, "he doesn't do anything all day."

She would have been eighty-nine years old last week, but she died on April Fools' Day. The joke is on me. I accepted the inevitable disintegration of age without realizing how bereaved her death would leave me. She was the last of my grandparents to die. Concetta was gone before I really knew her. Caesar left me with only the enduring feeling that it was possible to not have much money or education, and yet to be a gentleman to the starched tips of one's white shirt collar. My grandfather Eugene, the one who bested the natty Mr. LaForte, died when I was in college. He was often stern and always undemonstrative. I loved him blindly. I remember sitting at the kitchen table with him as he read my first newspaper story, a serviceable feature about someone's hundredth birthday. I watched him run his finger over my name, his name, at the top of the story, and I felt as though I might keel over with happiness.

Perhaps no four people have meant as much to me as they have, not only because they persuaded me that I had a past and a future, but because their affection and pride were rarely tinged with the perils of ownership. They were close enough to feel the satisfaction of blood in my successes, but not so close that my failures made them doubt themselves. This is the familiar dance of the generations, the minuet in which the closer we are the more difficult relations become. We are able to accept, even love, things in our grandparents that we find impossible to accept in their children, our parents. The reverse is true, too: in us they can take the joys without the responsibilities. In the family sandwich, the older people and the younger ones can recognize one another as the bread. Those in the middle are, for a time, the meat.

I realized this when I had children of my own. When I began to think of my father as my children's grandfather, I began to look at him differently. And he began to behave differently. During the summer he took my three-year-old fishing, a pursuit my father finds sacramental. It was a great rite of passage. But the ocean was rough, the boat dipped, plunged, rolled, and the little boy cried and turned pale. His grandfather turned back immediately to the quiet of the bay, not to embarrass the child by putting him ashore, but to find a quiet backwater where he could go crabbing and save face. It was a lovely thing done in a lovely fashion, and I am ashamed to say that I tried to cajole my son to remain out in the rough waters, for two reasons: I had more of my ego tied up in his behavior, and I could remember a small girl who didn't want to stay at sea, either, but whose father insisted she do so. That father is cut out to be a wonderful grandfather. He is funny, irreverent, rather eccentric, and a bit childish. He is a character.

My grandmother was a character, too. Despite the rosaries and the little clicking sound she made when someone told an off-color joke, she was no saint. I loved her for that. I never tired of hearing the story of my grandmother's career as a world-class shopper, of how one of my uncles was amazed to find himself first on line outside my grandmother's favorite department store the day of a big sale, then flabbergasted to hotfoot it up to the menswear department only to discover his mother peeking at him from the end of a rack of suits. Or the one about my parents bringing my grandmother home after a night on the town and trying to convince her that there was no place to get a nightcap at that hour. My grandmother grandly led them to the Irish War Veterans headquarters and knocked on the door. "Hello, Mrs. Quindlen," said the son of a friend she had known would be in charge that night. He let them in.

Now I am the meat in this family sandwich. Already, my elder son has invested his grandparents with a special aura; they are people who are very close to him in some magical way, but not too close for comfort. They get all the calls on his play telephone. That was what my grandparents always were to me.

"I'm going to be in heaven for my birthday," my grand-mother told her eldest daughter, who had tended her tirelessly as she weakened. "Sing 'Happy Birthday' to me." She had buried her husband and two of her children. She left two daughters, four sons, thirty-two grandchildren, twenty-nine great-grandchildren, and so many anecdotes that we were still telling them three hours after we left the cemetery. She always gave me the cherry from her Manhattan. In my mind, she'll live forever.

A
SICK
FRIEND

he way he told it, it really was a funny story. He was sitting at the kitchen table, his second beer in hand, talking about having minor surgery. He said the inside of the office looked like a gathering of ghosts, with the doctor and his assistants draped, masked, gowned, gloved. The trays, the floors, the chair, the countertops: everything was swathed in white. And there he was in the middle of it, feeling as though he should have a bell in his hand, so that when he could talk again he could clang the thing and cry "Unclean!"

You've got to trust me on this; he made us laugh at the whole thing. The time to cry was long past, the time when we all found out that he tested positive for the AIDS antibody, the beginning of the time when he knew that to have a mole removed or a tooth out would be a major undertaking, fraught with feelings of fear and anger and shame.

And then it got less funny. I noticed a deep

cut, and asked how he had gotten it. He had had an accident at home, but didn't go for stitches. He couldn't stand the idea of the fuss that would be made if he told them he was exposed. He couldn't stand how he would feel about himself if he didn't tell them.

And it stopped being funny at all when I came downstairs after he was gone and picked up my beer to finish it. And stared from the bottle in my hand to the bottle on the table and realized that I didn't know which was mine and which was his. And, feeling horrible, hypocritical, paranoid, pitched them both in the trash.

Things are bad all over on the AIDS front, even in our house, where we have routinely done what some of the folks of Arcadia, Florida, and Kokomo, Indiana, and a host of other towns went to extraordinary lengths to avoid. Our friend plays with our children, eats at our table, is never permitted to leave without a hug and a kiss on the cheek. It would never occur to me to do otherwise. I know I will not be exposed through him.

I know.

I think.

I hope.

I wanted to jump right on the people who have been bigoted about this, the people in Arcadia who wanted to keep those three little boys out of school and who refer to gay people as "queers," the ones in Kokomo who made Ryan White's life so unbearable that his family left town, the parents in Texas whose pediatrician closed up shop last week because his little patients were taken home when it turned out he was antibody positive. The people who won't eat at restaurants where gay waiters work or won't give blood. Except there is a little bit of them in all but the very best of us. We call them ignorant, and they are. But I suspect we all feel at least a little ignorant where AIDS is concerned.

The problem is that we would love absolute certainty on all aspects of this issue. We are a nation raised on True or False tests. We want doctors to give us the answers, which shows how short our memories are. After all, it was the doctors who told us that smoking wouldn't kill you and amphetamines during pregnancy didn't do a bit of harm. We want to know precisely how this disease spreads and why some people who are exposed get it and some don't and whether being exposed means inevitably getting sick. First we hear that the biggest argument against transmission through casual contact is that health-care workers don't get it. Then we hear that health-care workers have gotten it. And we don't know what to believe. All we know for sure is that getting sick means dying, at least so far. And that you can't get it from a beer bottle that's been sitting around for an hour. I know that.

I think.

I hope.

There is a very small cadre of smart and deeply committed people who have an unwavering commitment to never letting one small bit of the misinformation about this filter into their psyche. And there is a larger cadre of those who are using their poor children as an excuse to spout venom and lies about groups of people they despise and feel threatened by. And then there are a lot of people in the middle, people trying to be smart and rational about this, people who read the latest stories and statistics and try to be sensible and yet who watch a mosquito coming toward them and wonder where it's been and whose blood is inside it. When our friend first found out he had been exposed, he offered to stop visiting our house. I was indignant. What did he take me for? In medical parlance, it would be necessary for there to be "an exchange of bodily fluids" for him to infect my children. There was no risk to having him to dinner, more of a risk to cutting him out of our lives and depriving ourselves of his friendship and of our own self-esteem. So I smiled as he roughhoused with the older boy, and all the time somewhere in my mind I was thinking, "Please, God, don't let the kid accidentally bite him."

Columnists are usually in the business of opposites, of us and them. And that's what this started out being, a column about us and them. I continue to think about myself as different from people who torment first graders whose only crime was a bad blood transfusion, who are probably more likely to become mortally ill from well kids than the other way around. I continue to think of myself as different from those people who would leave a dying man on the sidewalk if he were bleeding in certain areas of New York and San Francisco. But I've watched the mosquitos on occasion, I must admit. And one night not too long ago I threw away the butt end of two perfectly good beers because one was mine and the other wasn't. Sometimes, when I'm feeling self-congratulatory, I think about that and I am ashamed, and I realize that maybe there is someplace between us and them, and that this is it.

GROWING
UP

GOOD GIRL, BAD GIRL

e met when we were both fifteen. She went to the beach with my family that summer, and when she stepped out of the bedroom we shared, wearing a two-piece bathing suit, I watched my father and one of his friends turn pale beneath their ruddy tans. As I lay on the beach in my own suit, its top boned into the facsimile of a bust, I could lift my head and through the gap between my sternum and the fabric see a sliver of gray-green water. For the first time in my life I was aware of sex, not the act, nor the mechanics, but the essence of it. And a gulf began to open between my friend and me.

But she was my best friend, and hard as it may have been to figure by the looks of us, she was the good girl, I the bad. I suppose everyone has at least one friendship like this in their lives. We were dialectical, she the thesis, I the antithesis. She was direct, trustworthy, kind, and naïve; I was manipulative, selfish, and clever. She laughed at all my jokes, took part in all my schemes, told everyone that I was the smartest and the funniest and the best. Like a B movie of boarding school life, we stole peanut butter from the refectory, short-sheeted beds, called drugstores and asked them if they had Prince Albert in a can. Whenever I hear a mother say, "If so-and-so told you to jump off the Brooklyn Bridge, would you do it?" I think of her. On my order, she would have jumped.

She hatched only one plot in all our time together, and it had such staggering simplicity that I leapt at it, sneaking down the fire escape in the middle of the night to meet our boyfriends at an all-night diner. It wasn't her fault that we got caught, that I got expelled, that she stayed on to become May Queen. It was the mid-sixties, so all we had done was to eat cheeseburgers and feel naughty. But as the bad girl I got the blame, and as the good girl she was assumed to have followed my lead. It was a time when good girls still got the breaks. It seemed terribly unfair then but seems exactly right now. And the gulf widened.

I went to a college that had a reputation, and she went to one with a football team. She was in the Midwest and I was in the Northeast. She cried when I told her I was on the pill, and she goggled at the suggestion that I was opposed to the war in Vietnam and wore overalls to class. I was a middle-of-the-road milquetoast at a school with its fair share of campus radicals, but she made me feel like Jane Fonda. I drove eight hours to her parents' home the summer after our freshman year to be the maid of honor at her wedding. Where she came from, a girl didn't wait for her B.A. to get her Mrs., particularly if the person who proposed was eager, older, and very rich. I wore purple organza and looked like an eggplant. There was a fountain full of whiskey sours. Within a year she had her first baby.

The seventies turned out to be a good time for bad girls, for the kind of girls who got A's in algebra and F's in conduct. I graduated from college and became a writer. I could always tell when she'd just had a haircut, because she'd call to say she'd seen one of my stories in a magazine in the beauty parlor. Right after one baby she had had another: son, daughter, daughter, son. Four children in seven years.

One night she called and asked me the kind of questions about life and love that you expect from your teenage sister, and I cried after we hung up. She was stunned when I got married, incredulous that a man with whom I had been living for years would buy the cow when he could get the milk for free. She sent me stationery with my new initials, not knowing I would not change my name. She and her husband flew in for the wedding in their private plane. The chasm was complete. A year went by before we spoke again.

Along came the eighties—a time of synthesis, thank God. No bad girls, no good girls, just women trying to get by as best they could. My friend finally stopped living in the past and I finally started paying attention to the present. She realized that she deserved more than the man to whom she was unhappily married, and I realized that I needed more than the work that I adored. She got divorced. I had a baby. She went back to college. I had another baby and quit my job. She got her bachelor's degree with honors, started the first real job she ever had, and moved away from the town where she was born. I worked hard to sink roots in the city I'd adopted, and went back to work part time. Last month we talked on the telephone for an hour about real estate, business clothes, family size, private schools, salary levels, divorce settlements, marriage, money, and men.

It's been almost twenty years now. Everything has changed. And yet some things never do. She never lost her figure. I never lost my edge. We've never been closer. In the last analysis, even at the best of times, there was never much more between us than love. But as the Beatles once said, it's all you need.

CITY KID

n the city neighborhood in which I live, stoop sitting is the primary summer spectator sport. One night, I found myself doing it with my father. Together we looked out on the vista of brick row houses, ten-family tenement buildings, and dozens of other stoops filled with other families. Across the street three elderly women were watching from their windows, pillows cushioning the sills; a group of men were fixing the transmission of a beaten-up Plymouth, and a wiffle-ball game was under way with pieces of corrugated cardboard box serving as bases.

My father leaned back and said philosophically, "Your grandfather worked hard all his life so that none of his grandchildren would ever have to live like this." I knew he was right. America is a country that loves lawns, and I have become a city kid. When my parents were growing up, success could be measured by how far you managed to travel from the tenements and the cement stoops. Lots of my friends have measured their success by whether they have managed to stay.

For many of us, these are the crunch years for setting up homes and setting down roots, when people dig in their heels or get out. In my neighborhood, the moving vans have been lumbering by like prehistoric beasts, dragging out antique bureaus and brass beds, taking them to places of grass and trees and lawn furniture.

These are places where the schools are good. The schools here aren't. Much of the green on our streets comes from glittery pieces of broken beer bottle. At 2:00 A.M. you can wake bolt upright to the sound of rap music coming from big shiny boxes with detachable speakers, music so loud it sounds as if it's coming from the clock radio next to the bed.

So people leave—usually for the sake of the children. You can open the door and let them outside and not worry that they'll be run over by beer trucks, these people say. You can let them go sledding in winter and swimming in summer and in between they can burn leaves at the curb and catch whirligigs that spin down from the maple trees and split them and stick them to the bridges of their noses. They can trick-or-treat and go caroling. There will be a basketball hoop at the end of every driveway.

It sounds wonderful. Perhaps my kids would love it. Certainly their father thinks they would. It's just not for me. I grew up in the suburbs; I know about catching lightning bugs and putting them in an empty peanut butter jar with holes punched in the top, and having a permanently scuffed place in your backyard where home plate always is. I'm not going to say it's sterile and awful, and dull people live there. That's not true. It's just that, like the perfectly nice guy you meet on a blind date who would be great for your friend Carol but could move to Indianapolis for all you care, the suburbs and I have no chemistry. The first time I walked down Broadway, something deep inside me just said "Yes."

My "Yes" should be subordinated to what is best for my children, according to one school of thought. I may actually spend a few grades in that school—if I decide that its opinion does not reflect a Tom Sawyer fantasy about children that is way off base. My children seem to like some of the same things about the city streets that I do: the people constantly eddying around them, the shifting play of color and movement, the 78-rpm metabolism in a 33⅓ world. Maybe they would prefer a yard, and the smell of the grass when it's just been mowed. There is a certain pathos to the fact that it is a big deal excursion for them to visit the lawn at the local college on the hill.

Those are the philosophical considerations. For lots of people we know, the decision to move has been financial. It's pretty chilling to discover that real estate is a primary determinant of family size in New York, and that the only-child phenomenon is to some extent a byproduct of the one-bedroom apartment. Some people have told me the only way they would have room for two is to move to the suburbs. Some simply said that they did not want to answer any more questions from their three-year-olds about why disheveled strangers were calling them Satan the Devil Incarnate the Son of Richard Nixon.

So someday the van may come to our house for what I can't help thinking of as the longest trip of our lives. My kids will play with other kids who are just like them, on streets that are just like ours and just like the one where I played with kids just like me. Perhaps my chemistry, my metabolism, will change. Not long ago my closest friend, who was a city person as sure as I was, moved to a place out in the suburbs for business reasons. We agreed that she'd have to tolerate it. Instead she bloomed. "It's so quiet and peaceful," she said happily over the phone. Exactly. That's my problem, right there.

MELTING POT

y children are upstairs in the house next door, having dinner with the Ecuadorian family that lives on the top floor. The father speaks some English, the mother less than that. The two daughters are fluent in both their native and their adopted languages, but the youngest child, a son, a close friend of my two boys, speaks almost no Spanish. His parents thought it would be better that way. This doesn't surprise me; it was the way my mother was raised, American among Italians. I always suspected, hearing my grandfather talk about the "No Irish Need Apply" signs outside factories, hearing my mother talk about the neighborhood kids, who called her greaseball, that the American fable of the melting pot was a myth. Here in our neighborhood it exists, but like so many other things, it exists only person-to-person.

The letters in the local weekly tabloid suggest that everybody hates everybody else here, and on a macro level they do. The old-timers are angry because they think the new moneyed professionals are taking over their town. The professionals are tired of being blamed for the neighborhood's rising rents, particularly since they are the ones paying them. The old immigrants are suspicious of the new ones. The new ones think the old ones are bigots. Nevertheless, on a micro level most of us get along. We are friendly with the Ecuadorian family, with the Yugoslavs across the street, and with the Italians next door, mainly by virtue of our children's sidewalk friendships. It took awhile. Eight years ago we were the new people on the block, filling dumpsters with old plaster and lath, drinking beer on the stoop with our demolition masks hanging around our necks like goiters. We thought we could feel people staring at us from behind the sheer curtains on their windows. We were right.

My first apartment in New York was in a gritty warehouse district, the kind of place that makes your parents wince. A lot of old Italians lived around me, which suited me just fine because I was the granddaughter of old Italians. Their own children and grandchildren had moved to Long Island and New Jersey. All they had was me. All I had was them.

I remember sitting on a corner with a group of half a dozen elderly men, men who had known one another since they were boys sitting together on this same corner, watching a glazier install a great spread of tiny glass panes to make one wall of a restaurant in the ground floor of an old building across the street. The men laid bets on how long the panes, and the restaurant, would last. Two years later two of the men were dead, one had moved in with his married daughter in the suburbs, and the three remaining sat and watched dolefully as people waited each night for a table in the restaurant. "Twenty-two dollars for a piece of veal!" one of them would say, apropos of nothing. But when I ate in the restaurant they never blamed me. "You're not one of them," one of the men explained. "You're one of me." It's an argument familiar to members of almost any embattled race or class: I like you, therefore you aren't like the rest of your kind, whom I hate.

Change comes hard in America, but it comes constantly. The butcher whose old shop is now an antiques store sits day after day outside the pizzeria here like a lost child. The old people across the street cluster together and discuss what kind of money they might be offered if the person who bought their building wants to turn it into condominiums. The greengrocer stocks yellow peppers and fresh rosemary for the gourmands, plum tomatoes and broad-leaf parsley for the older Italians, mangoes for the Indians. He doesn't carry plantains, he says, because you can buy them in the bodega.

Sometimes the baby slips out with the bath water. I wanted to throw confetti the day that a family of rough types who propped their speakers on their station wagon and played heavy metal music at 3:00 A.M. moved out. I stood and smiled as the seedy bar at the corner was transformed into a slick Mexican restaurant. But I liked some of the people who moved out at the same time the rough types did. And I'm not sure I have that much in common with the singles who have made the restaurant their second home.

Yet somehow now we seem to have reached a nice mix. About a third of the people in the neighborhood think of squid as calamari, about a third think of it as sushi, and about a third think of it as bait. Lots of the single people who have moved in during the last year or two are easygoing and good-tempered about all the kids. The old Italians have become philosophical about the new Hispanics, although they still think more of them should know English. The firebrand community organizer with the storefront on the block, the one who is always talking about people like us as though we stole our houses out of the open purse of a ninety-year-old blind widow, is pleasant to my boys.

Drawn in broad strokes, we live in a pressure cooker: oil and water, us and them. But if you come around at exactly the right time, you'll find members of all these groups gathered around complaining about the condition of the streets, on which everyone can agree. We melt together, then draw apart. I am the granddaughter of immigrants, a young professional—either an interloper or a longtime resident, depending on your concept of time. I am one of them, and one of us.

TUNING
FORKS

During our college years, I asked the man who is now my husband for the same gift for Valentine's Day, my birthday, and Christmas. He would say, "What do you want?" And I would reply, "An engagement ring." And he would laugh. In no time at all this became a standing joke, which is why, on my twenty-fifth birthday, I opened the latest in a succession of tiny boxes that had previously contained earrings, lockets, and the like with an air that was just a little bit lackadaisical. Inside the box was an engagement ring. Life had sneaked up behind me and planted a kiss on my cheek just as I had finally stopped straining to hear its footfalls. I wasn't looking for it, and so it came.

I know there are people who never strain, who go to look at houses they want to buy armed with a notebook, a list of practical questions, and a dignified, slightly critical manner. I know there are people who can argue about salary at job interviews and those who can greet a blind date—even one described by friends as a tall neurosurgeon with a great sense of humor—with a firm handshake and a level look.

And then there are people like me. I like to think of us as the tuning forks. When we are in the market for anything of substance—an apartment, a job, a relationship, a dress to wear on New Year's Eve—we give off a high-pitched tone akin to that emitted by dog whistles. This tone sends one of two messages to people: stay away, or take us for all we are worth. Most women have known a fair number of allegedly eligible men in each category (and some who started out in the second and then moved rapidly to the first). But of the rental agents and personnel managers I've known, most were the take-'em type. The only exception was the wonderful, cynical man who once interviewed me for a reporter's job and who, when I said I would work for free, answered coldly, "Don't be dramatic."

The tuning-fork phenomenon gives life an interesting quality, which, according to some friends, was introduced early in their own lives by their mothers. If you want something, it will elude you. If you do not want something, you will get ten of it in the mail. I have become such a firm believer in this that now that I have a place to live I half expect doormen all over New York City to dart forward as I pass by, grab my arm and say, "The penthouse just opened up—it has four bedrooms and a terrace, and the fireplace works."

This is in sharp contrast to the search for my first apartment, which took place with my pupils permanently dilated with desperation and desire, one of the telltale signs of tuning forks everywhere. I told agents that I didn't care if the bathtub was in the kitchen, didn't mind if there wasn't a kitchen at all, and thought the walk-in closet would indeed, with a little work, make a lovely bedroom. When I finally found a human habitation for rent, nothing could dissuade me. The delay on delivery of the refrigerator? (I'm getting a refrigerator? God! How great!) The hole in the bedroom ceiling? (I'll only see it when I'm lying down.) The rent? (It's reasonable. Or it would be if I had it. But I'll get it.)

Of course I adored that apartment because I had wanted it so badly, wanted it for no reason except that I was looking and it was there, which as many women can tell you is a key to some inexplicable and horrible relationships. During a time when I was in flux on just about every level, that apartment was my safe haven. I remember how, starting off from that apartment, I would take long walks around the city streets, in jeans and sneakers, buying flowers and food, window shopping, watching the pickup basketball games and the kids in the park. I thought this was all quite casual and continental, and that if I did it long enough I would meet some people. One morning a coworker said he had seen me walking the evening before and that he almost hadn't recognized me. "You looked so intense," he said. "You sort of looked like a cross between one of those kids with the big eyes in Keane paintings, and a serial murderer." No wonder I wasn't meeting anyone.

I was thinking about this the other night because of what happened on the bus. A man sat down next to me. I was reading my newspaper and he was reading his, and after a few minutes he started an idle conversation about some news event. That's when I noticed how handsome he was. In the course of the conversation, it also occurred to me that he was quite smart. When he asked if I had had dinner, I realized he was trying to pick me up.

Under other circumstances—say, if I had not had a husband and two small children at home waiting for me—this would have been marvelous, but under other circumstances this would not have happened. It crossed my mind that it was a function of age, that I was only so crazed when I was younger because I was younger, but I don't believe it's so. If I were still looking, that man would have changed seats or feigned sleep or keeled over in a fake faint rather than talk to me. He would have heard the hum. He would have known that he could tell me he'd like to have dinner, but wanted to warn me that he was leaving the next day to join the Green Berets for a secret training mission in Lebanon, and that in response I would have said only two words: "Which restaurant?"

A L O N E
A T
L A S T

got in a lot of trouble when I was a kid for not getting enough fresh air. There was a big chair in our living room, overstuffed and worn, and even on the nicest day of the year I could be found there, my legs draped over one arm of the chair, reading. I read a great deal, with no particular sense of originality or discernment. I read the Hardy Boys and Nancy Drew, C. S. Lewis and Robert Louis Stevenson, *A Little Princess* and *A Wrinkle in Time.* I read pretty awful stuff, like teen magazines, and I read pretty adult stuff, like *Wuthering Heights.* I still remember reading *Ulysses* when I was thirteen and thinking "What a weird book."

My mother was thinking "What a weird child." When the sun was shining and the neighborhood kids were playing Monkey in the Middle, my mother was always yelling at me to go outside and get some fresh air. She did not think it was healthy to stay inside and read so much. One summer, to force me into the great outdoors, I was sent to camp in the mountains. Thinking of it even today is, as Evelyn Waugh's Bright Young Things say, "too, too sick-making." All those people and all that activity all the time: my God, I'll never forget it.

I still read constantly: if my kids ever go into analysis, I'm sure they will say they don't really remember my face because it was always hidden by a book. Obviously this is in part because I like books. But another reason is that I like to be alone. I like to go deep inside myself and not be accompanied there by anyone else. But I am the oldest of five children, and when I was young I had about as much chance of being alone as I did of being a lion tamer. Reading was for me then a way of lifting myself out of a crowded environment into a place where I could be by myself. No wonder my mother was concerned. Being by yourself was considered, at my age and in my family, an aberrant behavior. Camp was normal. Camp was fun. Camp was crowded. Camp was horrible.

We pay lip service to a notion that privacy is important, but I don't really think we believe it much. When anyone lives alone we have a tendency to think they are just waiting to meet the right roommate; we have an impulse to pair our friends off or introduce them to others. Single people eating in restaurants are assumed to be there for lack of a companion, not because they like their own company. It is difficult for us to accept that a great many gregarious people are often, also, quite private inside, that they have a chocolate-covered almond kind of character. This happens to be the case with me, although societal conditioning has made me think about these two parts of myself as a little like the geography of the state of Michigan. I am so gregarious that I once went to an Irish wake and was the perfect mourner, even though I realized when I approached the casket that I was in the wrong viewing room. And I love solitude so much that easily one of my favorite parts of the week is when I have somehow finished my work before the sitter is due to leave and I can hide out in my room for half an hour and read a Lord Peter Wimsey mystery.

Actually when I lived alone I was lonely a fair amount of the time, but it felt somehow restorative. Perhaps I was making up for all those years of living in a crowded house, and all the years to come when, I suspected, I would live in one again. Because of youth or duty or love I have most often lived in crowded houses, in which a book was partly an excuse for staring into the middle distance, zoning out, being inside your own skin. I have cultivated pastimes that make this kind of behavior socially acceptable. I do needlework, watch television, and, yes, read—all excuses for chewing the cud, ruminating over whatever crosses my mental screen. Or, like a narcoleptic, I can simply lapse into my middle distance attitude. My eyes unfocus and my mouth drops open just a bit. I look like a fish who has just been sideswiped by the *QE II* and never knew what hit it. My family calls this my "zone look." It means *do not disturb*.

I wonder if this is hereditary, or whether I simply belong to a family made up of essentially solitary people placed by fate within large and voluble groups. My father, for example, fishes; it is a pursuit some people don't understand, luring a stupid cold-blooded animal to its death on the end of a piece of string. But fishing has very little to do with fish, at least the way my dad practices it. It has to do with sinking within yourself, charting your course. And I'm all for that.

I also have a child who habitually lapses into the zone look, although at his age I cannot imagine what he is thinking. Friends have started to ask me when he will begin lessons: swimming, piano, art, and the like. I want him to have the best of everything, but the best of everything for me was often staring off into the middle distance. I want him to have lots of time for that. If I were asked what I am most afraid of his missing in life, I think I would answer "Solitude." I would say the same for me.

RAISED
ON
ROCK-AND-ROLL

ister Ed is back on television, indicating that, as most middle-of-the-road antique shops suggest, Americans cannot discriminate between things worth saving and things that simply exist. *The Donna Reed Show* is on, too, and *My Three Sons,* and those dopey folks from *Gilligan's Island.* There's *Leave It to Beaver* and *The Beverly Hillbillies* and even *Lassie,* whose plaintive theme song leaves my husband all mushy around the edges.

Social historians say these images, and those of Howdy Doody and Pinky Lee and Lamb Chop and Annette have forever shaped my consciousness. But I have memories far stronger than that. I remember sitting cross-legged in front of the tube, one of the console sets with the ersatz lamé netting over the speakers, but I was not watching puppets or pratfalls. I was born in Philadelphia, a city where if you can't dance you might as well stay home, and I was raised on rock-and-roll. My earliest television memory is of *American Bandstand,* and the central question of my childhood was: Can you dance to it?

When I was fifteen and a wild devotee of Mitch Ryder and the Detroit Wheels, it sometimes crossed my mind that when I was thirty-four years old, decrepit, wrinkled as a prune and near death, I would have moved on to some nameless kind of dreadful show music, something akin to Muzak. I did not think about the fact that my parents were still listening to the music that had been popular when they were kids; I only thought that they played "Pennsylvania 6-5000" to torment me and keep my friends away from the house.

But I know now that I'm never going to stop loving rock-and-roll, all kinds of rock-and-roll: the Beatles, the Rolling Stones, Hall and Oates, Talking Heads, the Doors, the Supremes, Tina Turner, Elvis Costello, Elvis Presley. I even like really bad rock-and-roll, although I guess that's where my age shows; I don't have the tolerance for Bon Jovi that I once had for the Raspberries.

We have friends who, when their son was a baby, used to put a record on and say, "Drop your butt, Phillip." And Phillip did. That's what I love: drop-your-butt music. It's one of the few things left in my life that makes me feel good without even thinking about it. I can walk into any bookstore and find dozens of books about motherhood and love and human relations and so many other things that we once did through a combination of intuition and emotion. I even heard recently that some school is giving a course on kissing, which makes me wonder if I'm missing something. But rock-and-roll flows through my veins, not my brain. There's nothing else that feels the same to me as, say, the faint sound of the opening dum-doo-doo-doo-doo-doo of "My Girl" coming from a radio on a summer day. I feel the way I felt when I first heard it. I feel good, as James Brown says.

There are lots of people who don't feel this way about

rock-and-roll. Some of them don't understand it, like the Sen-
ate wives who said that records should have rating stickers on
them so that you would know whether the lyrics were dirty.
The kids who hang out at Mr. Big's sub shop in my neighborhood thought this would make record shopping a lot easier,
because you could choose albums by how bad the rating was.
Most of the people who love rock-and-roll just thought the
labeling idea was dumb. Lyrics, after all, are not the point of
rock-and-roll, despite how beautifully people like Bruce Springsteen and Joni Mitchell write. Lyrics are the point only in the
case of "Louie, Louie"; the words have never been deciphered,
but it is widely understood that they are about sex. That's
understandable, because rock-and-roll is a lot like sex: If you
talk seriously about it, it takes a lot of the feeling away—and
feeling is the point.

Some people over-analyze rock-and-roll, just as they over-
analyze everything else. They say things like "Bruce Springsteen is the poet laureate of the American dream gone sour,"
when all I need to know about Bruce Springsteen is that the
saxophone bridge on "Jungleland" makes the back of my neck
feel exactly the same way I felt the first time a boy kissed me,
only over and over and over again. People write about Prince's
"psychedelic masturbatory fantasies," but when I think about
Prince, I don't really think, I just feel—feel the moment when,
driving to the beach, I first heard "Kiss" on the radio and
started bopping up and down in my seat like a seventeen-year-
old on a day trip.

I've got precious few things in my life anymore that just
make me feel, that make me jump up and dance, that make
me forget the schedule and the job and the mortgage payments
and just let me thrash around inside my skin. I've got precious
few things I haven't studied and considered and reconsidered
and studied some more. I don't know a chord change from a
snare drum, but I know what I like, and I like feeling this way

sometimes. I love rock-and-roll because in a time of talk, talk, talk, it's about action.

Here's a test: Get hold of a two-year-old, a person who has never read a single word about how heavy-metal musicians should be put in jail or about Tina Turner's "throaty alto range." Put "I Heard It Through the Grapevine" on the stereo. Stand the two-year-old in front of the stereo. The two-year-old will begin to dance. The two-year-old will drop his butt. Enough said.

CHRISTMAS

e will have a cold antipasto and chicken parmigiana for dinner tonight. I could have told you this a week ago. I could have told you this in March. It is an Italian tradition to feast on Christmas Eve, to crowd the table with calamari and scungilli, bacalla and pieces of fried eel.

But my husband does not eat any of those traditional dishes, so I have adapted the menu. Afterward we will read "A Christmas Carol," alternating chapters. I realized years ago that he got the best chapters. He gets the first, gets to intone, "Marley was dead, to begin with." And he gets the last, so that at the end he can say, "God bless us every one!" But it has always been so. It is too late to change now.

Christmas is the mainstay of my year because tradition is the mainstay of my life. It keeps me whole. It is the centrifugal force that stops the pieces from shooting wildly into the void. The only way I can bear the changes that grind on inexorably around me is to pepper the year with those things that never change. Bath and books for the boys before bedtime. Homemade cakes on their birthdays. The beach in August. Chestnuts roasting on an open fire. Jack Frost nipping at your nose. You name it, I do it.

We buy our tree at the same lot every year. "Where's the biggest tree you've got?" I ask, and as though he knows just what I need, the man who runs the place repeats the same performance every year, looks askance and says, "The biggest?" Then we grin at each other, because we know he will never find a tree higher than the ceiling in the corner of our high-ceilinged Victorian parlor—the traditional place for our tree. It will be decorated, not with any kind of theme or special color, just the hodgepodge of glass balls, pressed tin ornaments, and little stuffed figures I've collected over the years. Each year I buy two new ones.

It turns out that this is the sort of person I am. For a long time I wondered, but now I am sure. Sometimes I dreamed of moving on the spur of the moment to Paris, of throwing a pair of black velvet pants and a black silk shirt and some jeans and a T-shirt into a satchel and setting up shop on the rue de Something, writing poetry and dancing till dawn until another fancy struck me. But I never was that kind of person, and I never will be. Perhaps I realized this the first Christmas that I was free, alone, mistress of my own three rooms on the top floor of a little brick townhouse in a city so big no one would know if I missed Mass because I was sleeping one off. And I rounded up the children of my friends and set out little bowls of colored frosting and made them decorate cookies with me. And I dragged home a pathetic little tree and hung the cookies on it. And I went to midnight Mass at the church around the corner and hung my stocking on my mantel and stuffed things in it the next morning. And took the bus home to my family.

I will never jump on the next plane to Paris, never travel

light. I often envy people who can. Their lives seem more exciting to me, less calcified. I am sure that they have unlimited opportunities to re-create themselves, and that they do. I look at Madonna, who was untidy in lace and bracelets last year and this year is sleek in black bustiers and an elegant cap of bleached hair, and think how exhilarating it must be to be that, to be someone new each time you turn around.

I'm not like that. The question of moving the tree this year from one end of the living room to the other is of enormous moment. The idea of getting a slightly smaller, more practical one is simply not to be borne. I will always need my sampler with the Irish blessing, the mirror from my mother's bureau, my appliqué quilt, the complete Dickens I bought at a flea market for two dollars when I was fifteen, yuletide carols being sung by a choir, folks dressed up like Eskimos.

Sometimes this makes oil and water of my life: getting married in Alençon lace and pearls, and yet keeping my own name; answering all my sons' questions absolutely truthfully, and then assuring them that Santa does exist; questioning church teachings in my mind, and yet reading the Christmas Gospel in church and feeling the power of its message in my heart: "And she brought forth her firstborn son, and wrapped him in swaddling clothes, and laid him in a manger." The echo I hear is the sound of the years passing: a little girl in a navy-blue wool coat with a velvet collar, a teenager in a camel's-hair coat with big bone buttons, a woman in fur, in tears, enamored of the ridiculous notion that some things need never change, that some things are safe, holding the hand of her firstborn son in the blood-red shadows of stained glass.

I know who I am. I am these things: the trip to see the tree at Rockefeller Center, the plaster Santa with a spray of holly in his chimney, the Advent calendar, its last door open to reveal the Nativity. I spend a good deal of time looking at Advent calendars, and was finally satisfied with this one, only to open the first door and realize with a rush of memory, like a sudden sneeze, that it was the same one I chose last year. I suppose that is just right, too. I need eternal verities—otherwise I worry that there are no verities. When I consider it in the abstract, it sometimes seems boring, odd, and old. But in real life it is, well, real life. A cold antipasto. Chicken parmigiana. I have done it before. I will do it again. Although it's been said, many times, many ways, merry Christmas to you.

MONSTERS

The monster under the bed finally arrived at our house the other night. I've been waiting for him to show up for four years. *Peter Rabbit* had been read, discussed, analyzed, and placed on the floor for easy access. The little brother was coiled under his blankets, waiting to leap out and seize forbidden tow trucks and alphabet blocks as soon as the sound of the parents going downstairs had faded to a faint thump. The bathtub faucet was drip drip dripping in the next room. The drinks of water had been parceled out, demanded again, refused. The overhead light was off. The night-light gleamed.

"Mom?"

"Yes."

"I have something very important to tell you."

"What?"

"There is a monster under my bed."

Do you have any idea how close I came to replying, "Well, it's about time."

Lord, it seems like the monster first showed up under my bed just the day before yesterday. I always figured he was a hairy guy, with a lot of teeth, a cross between Godzilla and a Gahan Wilson drawing. He never got me, but that was because I was quick and brave and careful. After I finished reading in bed I went across to the switch next to the door and turned out the light. Then I hoisted my nightgown up to my knobby knees, took a deep breath, ran three steps and leapt up onto the mattress. Don't break stride. Don't look down. I didn't need to; I knew that if I had eyes in my chin I'd see a long nasty arm whipping out to grab me by the ankle and pull me under. Beneath the bedspread I was safe. One more night alive.

What did I tell the kid about his monster? Something lame, I think, like, "Would Daddy and I let monsters in this house?" Followed by a rambling discussion of things that are there and things you only think are there and their relative dangers and merits. (The last time we had this discussion it was because he didn't want to sleep in the top bunk. "The things on the ceiling go in my ears." "Honey, those are shadows." Long explanation about shadows, how shadows form, the benign nature of shadows. The next night he still does not want to sleep on the top bunk. "The shadows on the ceiling go in my ears." Fast learner.)

I knew what I was supposed to say. I was supposed to say there aren't any monsters under the bed, to get down on my hands and knees and peer underneath and get him to join me for confirmation and solace. Which doesn't do a bit of good because they come back as soon as you douse the lights, as any child knows. But I somehow couldn't bring myself to flatly deny the monster. I have a lot of trouble with those rare times when, for good reason, I lie to my children. For instance, I've been tormented by Santa Claus. Here I go, telling the truth: Do all people die? Will the needle hurt? Do you love Christopher? Yes. Yes. Yes. And suddenly one day I unequivocally confirm that a fat man is coming down the chimney to leave toys, eat the cookies, drink the milk, and get to his cousin Kate's house forty miles away before daybreak. Of course, I did this—I'm not one of those modern moms with angular etchings on my walls who thinks Santa is an irrational vestige of anachronistic religious festivals—but it felt funny to me, telling him Santa is real when he really isn't, and when he'll find out some day that he isn't.

That's why I can't deny the monster, tell him that nothing is under the bed. Because I believe in monsters, and someday my kid will believe in them even more surely than he does now. My mother lied. (My mother once even put a dust ruffle on the bed. Can you imagine? Giving aid and sustenance to the monsters! That lasted three days.) When you grow up you realize that there isn't really any Santa but the monsters are still around. If only they were big and hairy; now they're just dark and amorphous, and they're no longer afraid of the light. Sometimes they're the guy who climbs in the window and takes your television. And sometimes they're the guy who walks out the front door with your heart in his hand and never comes back. And sometimes they're the job or the bank or the wife or the boss or just that sort of dark heavy feeling that sits between your shoulder blades like a backpack. There are always terrible things waiting to grab you by the ankle, to pull you under, to get you with their long horrible arms. And you lie in bed and look at the shadows on the ceiling and feel, under the covers, just for a moment, like you're safe. One more day alive.

I'm feeling my way on the monster, now that he's finally arrived. I should have had an answer for this one all cooked up, but then I wouldn't be a mom but a magician. Make a game out of it. Tame the monster. Give him a name and some habits and maybe even a family. Leave a Tootsie Roll pop on the floor to buy the monster's friendship. (The little brother, wild as a punk haircut, will be out of bed and unwrapping that sucker before the parents make it to the first landing.) Or maybe this is one of those times when I should simply leave the kid to his own devices. After all, some things you get taught. And some things you just learn.

ANNA QUINDLEN created her "Life inthe 30's" column for *The New York Times* in 1986. It is now syndicated throughout the country. A 1974 graduate of Barnard College, she was a reporter and editor at the *Times* from 1977–1985, first as a general assignment and City Hall reporter, then as the author of the "About New York" column, and finally as the deputy metropolitan editor. She lives with her husband and their two sons in New Jersey and is at work on her first novel, to be published by Random House.